...ttire

CLOSE-FITTING CLOTHES

LONG PANTS

THICK-SOLED SHOES PREFERABLY WITH STEEL TOES

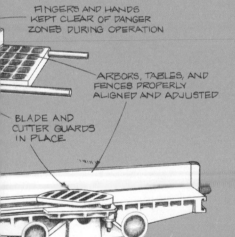

FINGERS AND HANDS KEPT CLEAR OF DANGER ZONES DURING OPERATION

ARBORS, TABLES, AND FENCES PROPERLY ALIGNED AND ADJUSTED

BLADE AND CUTTER GUARDS IN PLACE

POWER TOOLS NEVER LEFT RUNNING UNATTENDED

Safety Tools

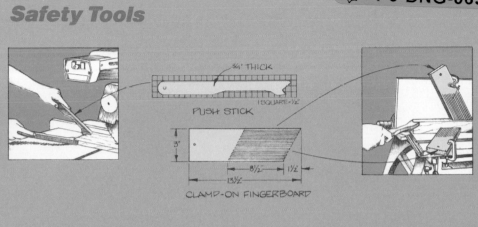

¾" THICK

PUSH STICK

1 SQUARE = ½"

3"

13½"

8½"

1½"

CLAMP-ON FINGERBOARD

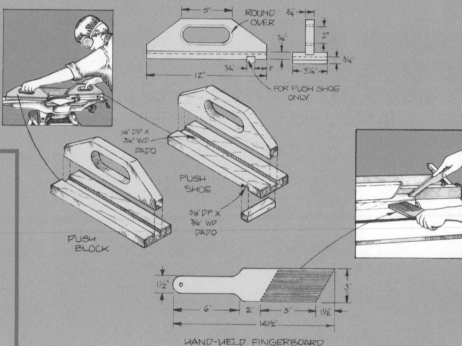

5"

ROUND OVER

¾"

2"

¾"

12"

¾"

1"

3¼"

¾"

FOR PUSH SHOE ONLY

¼" DP X ¾" WD DADO

PUSH SHOE

⅜" DP X ¾" WD DADO

PUSH BLOCK

1½"

6"

2"

5"

1½"

14½"

3"

HAND-HELD FINGERBOARD

In Case of Emergency

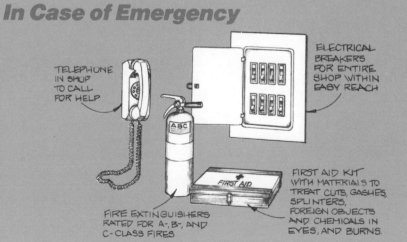

TELEPHONE IN SHOP TO CALL FOR HELP

ELECTRICAL BREAKERS FOR ENTIRE SHOP WITHIN EASY REACH

ABC

FIRST AID

FIRE EXTINGUISHERS RATED FOR A-, B-, AND C-CLASS FIRES

FIRST AID KIT WITH MATERIALS TO TREAT CUTS, GASHES, SPLINTERS, FOREIGN OBJECTS AND CHEMICALS IN EYES, AND BURNS.

·BUILD·IT·BETTER·YOURSELF·
WOODWORKING PROJECTS

Weekend Projects

Collected and Written
by Nick Engler

Rodale Press
Emmaus, Pennsylvania

If you have any questions or comments concerning this book, please write:
Rodale Press
Book Reader Service
33 East Minor Street
Emmaus, PA 18098

Series Editor: Jeff Day
Managing Editor/Author: Nick Engler
Editor: Roger Yepsen
Copy Editor: Mary Green
Graphic Designer: Linda Watts
Graphic Artists: Christine Vogel
                 Chris Walendzak
Photography: Karen Callahan
Cover Photography: Mitch Mandel
Cover Photograph Stylist: Janet C. Vera
Proofreader: Hue Park
Typesetting by Computer Typography, Huber Heights, Ohio
Interior Illustrations by Mary Jane Favorite, Scot T. Marsh, and
  O'Neil & Associates, Dayton, Ohio
Endpaper Illustrations by Mary Jane Favorite
Produced by Bookworks, Inc., West Milton, Ohio

Library of Congress Cataloging-in-Publication Data

Engler, Nick.
    Weekend projects / collected and written by Nick Engler.
        p.   cm. — (Build-it-better-yourself woodworking
    projects)
    ISBN 0-87857-941-9   hardcover
    ISBN 0-87857-942-7   paperback
    1. Woodwork.   I. Title.   II. Series: Engler, Nick. Build-it-
better-yourself woodworking projects.
TT180.E65   1991
684'.08—dc20   90-46392
                                                                  CIP

Distributed in the book trade by St. Martin's Press

 4 6 8 10 9 7 5   hardcover
2 4 6 8 10 9 7 5 3 1 paperback

Contents

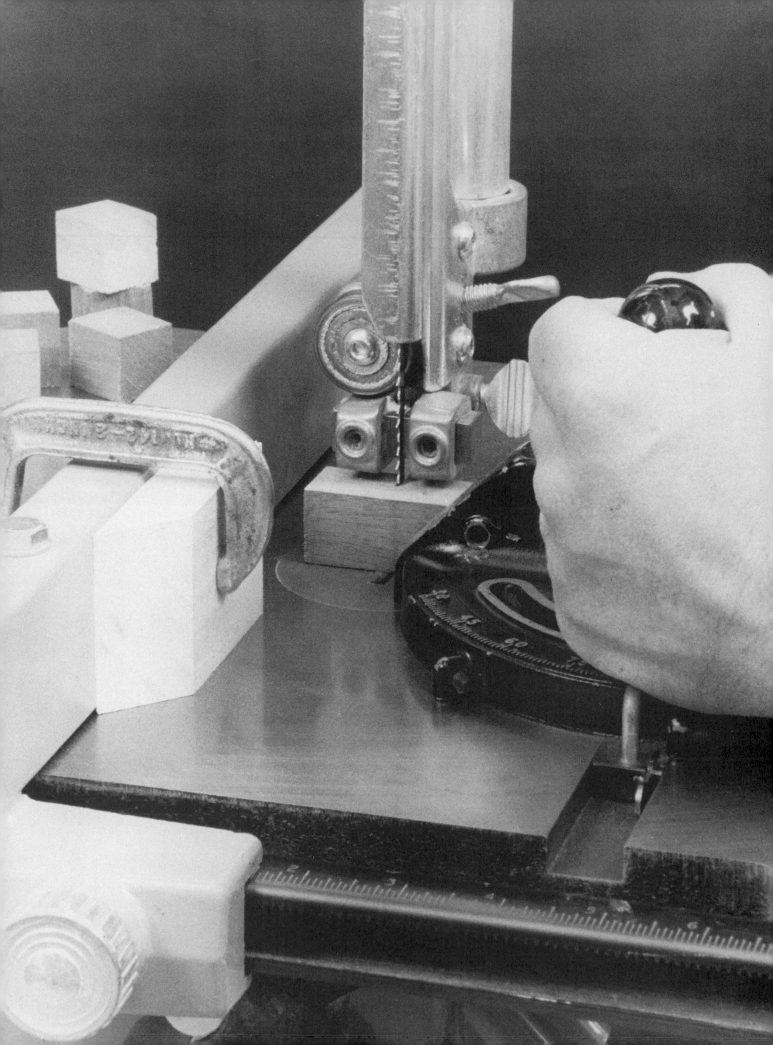

Shortcuts

An optimistic how-to writer once boasted, "Any project can be a weekend project if you know enough shortcuts."

Unfortunately, this isn't quite true. Even with a skilled crew, it would be impossible to put a highboy, a house, or an aircraft carrier together in a weekend. However, knowing a few simple shortcuts can significantly shorten the time it takes to complete a project — *any* project — without sacrificing quality.

Planning Ahead

Perhaps the biggest shortcut is the most obvious — *plan ahead*. Think through your project before you build it, planning the sequence of cuts and other operations in order to use as few tool setups as possible. In several time management studies, researchers found that cabinetmakers spent over *half* of their time in setting up the tools. The actual woodworking — cutting, drilling, shaping, and so on — took less than one-tenth of the total time invested in each project. Consequently, if you can reduce the number of setups you have to make, you can reduce the time it takes to make a project.

That is why the instructions for each project in this book advise you to cut all the parts to size *first*. Most novice woodworkers cut the parts as they go, custom-fitting each to the assembly. This wastes time because you set up the table saw, jointer, and planer for each cut. It's much more time-efficient if you do *all* the planing, *all* the jointing and ripping, and *all* the crosscutting in three consecutive operations at the beginning of the project.

Once you have cut the parts, try to arrange the remaining operations so you switch tools and setups as little as possible. For example, drill all the holes needed in a project in a single, unbroken sequence. Start with the large holes and work your way to the smaller ones, or the other way around. You'll be done with the drill press setups and won't have to keep going back to the tool to make a few holes here and there.

Stop Blocks

After you've thought through the project and begun woodworking, take advantage of jigs and fixtures to speed your progress. Perhaps the most useful time-saving jig is the simple *stop block*. This is just a small piece of wood, beveled on one end, that clamps to any fence, extension, or straightedge.

Use a stop block to *duplicate* an operation, rather than measure and mark several parts. Stop blocks are most commonly used to saw duplicate lengths of wood. (See Figure 1.) However, you can also use them for a variety of joinery and drilling operations. They will help you to duplicate the length of mortises and tenons, the locations of dadoes, the spacing of holes, and so on. (See Figures 2 and 3.)

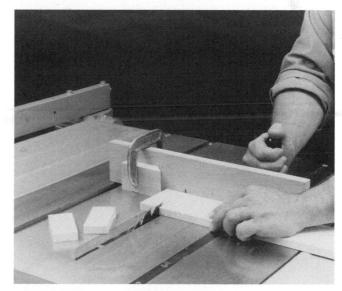

1/Clamp a stop block to the fence of a table saw to cut duplicate lengths of wood. Note that the wood butts against the *beveled* end. This frees you from having to brush the sawdust out of the way between each cut.

Pad Operations

When you can't use a stop block to duplicate parts or joints, you may be able to use a *pad* — a stack of boards. These must be secured so they won't shift as you machine them. You can employ several methods to keep the pad together — clamps, finishing nails, masking tape, or, easiest of all, double-faced carpet tape. It's remarkably strong and doesn't leave any holes in the stock. Also, you don't have to retape edges as you cut them, as you do when using masking tape. (See Figure 4.)

Saw the pad, drill it, or sand it as needed. If you're sawing shapes, sand the sawed edges before taking the pad apart. When you've done all the operations you need to do, remove the clamps, nails, or tape. (See Figures 5 and 6.)

Extra Parts

Some parts are "heavily machined." That is, they go through several different steps before they're completely shaped. For example, to make a door stile from a board, you must cut it to size, cut a panel groove or glass rabbet, make mortises or dowel joints at each end, and finally chisel recesses for the hinges or drill a hole for pull. If you make a mistake during any one of these operations, you may have to go back several steps and make a new stile.

To save yourself the time it takes to repeat all these tool setups and operations, make one or two extra copies of heavily machined parts as you go. Then, if you make a mistake, you have a ready-made replacement. The time this saves will far outweigh the extra expense in wood.

Sharpening

One of the most overlooked shortcuts is to sharpen tools *frequently*. Novice woodworkers tend to press on through a project with dull blades and cutters, more intent on the work than the condition of their tools. Experienced cabinetmakers often sharpen their tools at the beginning of a major project, then *touch up the edges* with a whetstone or file now and then as they work. (See Figure 7.) This not only saves time but also increases the accuracy of the work.

Clean Up

Another frequently overlooked shortcut is to clean up *as you work*. Get in the habit of hanging up hand tools or putting away materials when you finish using them — even though you expect to use them again in a few

2/Use a stop block to gauge the length of a tenon as you cut it. Clamp the block to a miter gauge extension.

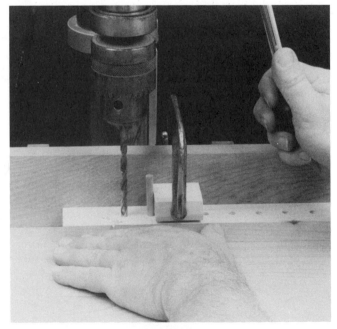

3/In this drill press setup, the stop block helps to space holes evenly. Drill a hole, put a peg in it, and slide the board sideways until the peg hits the stop block. Drill another hole, take the peg out of the first hole and put it in the one you just drilled, and repeat.

minutes. Many novice woodworkers let tools and materials collect on their workbenches, thinking this will save the time it takes to get them out again. Far from saving time, they waste it as they constantly rearrange the clutter to make room for the work.

You can make it much easier to clean up as you work by arranging your shop so all the frequently used tools and materials are *near at hand*. Design and build a workbench with several different types of storage — drawers, shelves, racks — and lots of it.

4/When stacking boards to make duplicate parts, use double-faced carpet tape to stick the "pad" together.

Press down firmly to get a good bond. You may want to clamp the parts together briefly.

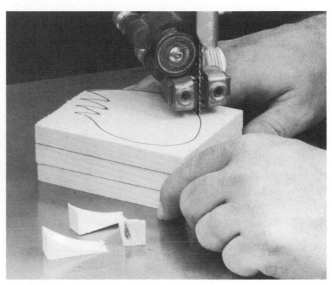

5/Duplicate irregular shapes by sawing several boards stacked face to face to make a pad.

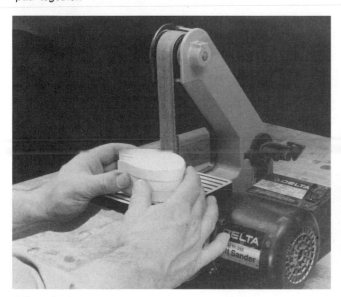

6/Once you've sawed the shapes, drill holes and sand the sawed edges as needed. After you finish all the necessary operations, take the pad apart.

7/Keep a whetstone handy and touch up the cutting edges of your tools occasionally as you work. Diamond whetstones make good touch-up stones. They will sharpen a variety of tool-steel edges, including carbide. And they don't have to be oiled constantly — just wash off the "swarf" (filings) now and then with water.

Shaker Clock

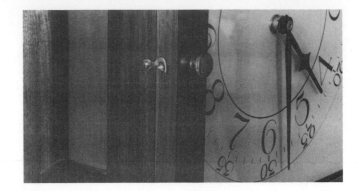

On May 12, 1840, Brother Isaac Young, a member of the New Lebanon Shaker Community in New York State, completed his twenty-first clock. It was a wall clock, designed to be hung on a peg rail. Inside the case, he wrote the date and clock number, as well as these lines:

O' Time! how swift that solemn day rolls on when from these mortal scenes we shall be gone!

The clock case shown is a reproduction of Brother Young's nineteenth-century design. The clockwork, however, is a modern battery-powered movement. The pendulum is electrically driven, and the chimes are produced electronically. This helps make the clock relatively simple and inexpensive to build. However, the clock still looks and sounds like the old Shaker original.

Materials List

FINISHED DIMENSIONS

PARTS

A. Sides (2) $5/8'' \times 41/2'' \times 343/4''$
B. Top/bottom $5/8'' \times 55/8'' \times 14''$
C. Divider $5/8'' \times 21/4'' \times 123/4''$
D. Back $1/2'' \times 12'' \times 39''$
E. Door rails/top
       door stiles (6) $1/2'' \times 11/4'' \times 123/4''*$
F. Bottom door
       stiles (2) $1/2'' \times 11/4'' \times 213/8''*$
G. Face mount
       rails (2) $3/8'' \times 11/2'' \times 12''$
H. Face mount
       stiles (2) $3/8'' \times 11/2'' \times 123/4''$
J. Speaker mount
       (optional) $3/8'' \times 27/8'' \times 3''$

*Cut the door stiles to this length, assemble the frames, **then** plane the doors to fit.*

HARDWARE

Clock movement with 20″–24″
    pendulum
Metal or hardboard clock face with
    8½″–10″ dia. time ring (face must be
    no less than 10¼″ square)
⅝″ dia. Brass door pulls (2)
Small brass hooks (2)
#2 x ½″ Brass roundhead screws (8)
4d Cut nails (12–16)
⅛″ x 10⅝″ x 10⅝″ Glass pane
⅛″ x 10⅝″ x 19¼″ Glass pane
½″ Wire brads (10–12)
2¼″ x 7¼″ Hopsack cloth
Upholstery tacks (12–16)

EXPLODED VIEW

1 Select the clock movement, face, and hands.

The clock case shown can be adapted to hold either electronic or mechanical movements. When choosing a movement, your only constraints are that the pendulum should be 20″–24″ long (as measured from the hand shaft to the center of the bob), and the swing (side-to-side motion of the bob) should be no more than 8. (Some electronic movements come with long pendulums that can be trimmed to any length. The movement in this clock came with a 28″-long pendulum, which was shortened to 22″.) We purchased a battery-powered electronic movement for several reasons:

- It's slightly less expensive than comparable mechanical movements.
- It's easier to mount.
- It doesn't need winding or maintenance — just replace the battery every year.
- New technology has made most electronic chimes almost indistinguishable from mechanical chimes.

After selecting a movement, choose a clockface and hands to fit it. The time dial on the clockface should be 8½″–10″ in diameter, and the hands must fit the dial. The face should be printed on metal or thin hardboard, and should measure at least 10¼″ square. (You can use a paper face if you mount it on ⅛″-thick hardboard.) Many clock supply companies offer reproductions of Shaker clock parts. If these aren't available in the proper size, choose a simple Regulator-style clockface and hands. Here are several sources:

Heirloom Clocks
Craft Products Company
2200 Dean Street
St. Charles, IL 60174

Klockit
P.O. Box 636
Lake Geneva, WI 53147

Mason & Sullivan
586 Higgins Crowell Road
West Yarmouth, MA 02673

2 If necessary, adjust the dimensions of the clock case.

Wait until you've purchased the clock movement *and have it in hand* before selecting the wood or cutting any parts. Measure the dimensions of the movement and note how it mounts in the case. (Most electronic movements attach to the clockface; mechanical movements bolt to the back or a special mounting board.) As designed, the height and width of this clock case should accommodate all movements, both electronic and mechanical. The depth is sufficient for most electronic movements. However, you'll probably have to make the case deeper for mechanical movements. To do this, increase the width of the sides, top, and bottom by the same amount.

Note: You may also have to increase the depth of the case if you've purchased an electronic movement with an external speaker larger than 2½″ in diameter.

3 Select the stock and cut it to size.

To build the clock case as designed, you need about 10 board feet of 4/4 (four-quarters) cabinet-grade lumber. Both the original case that Brother Young built in 1840 and this copy were made from walnut. However, Shaker clockmakers also used cherry, maple, and white pine.

When you have selected the wood, glue up stock to make the 12″-wide back. Plane the wood to ⅝″ thick and cut the top, bottom, sides, and divider to size. Plane the remaining wood to ½″ thick and cut the door rails, door stiles, and back. Cut 2 or 3 extra door rails so you can test the machine setups when you make the joinery. Then, once again, plane the remaining wood — this time to ⅜″ thick. Cut the face mount rails, face mount stiles, and speaker mount. Make one or two extra rails.

Note: You'll need a speaker mount only if you've bought an electronic movement with an external speaker. If not, omit this part.

4

Cut the joinery in the sides. The divider, face mount, and back all rest in dadoes, rabbets, or grooves cut in the sides. Using a router or dado cutter, make a ½"-wide, ¼"-deep rabbet in the back edge of each side as shown in the *Side Layout*. Also cut a ³⁄₈"-wide, ¼"-deep, 12¾"-long blind groove, starting at the top end. Finally, make a ⅝"-wide, ¼"-deep, 1⅛"-long blind dado, starting at the front edge. This dado joins the groove to form a dogleg. The easiest way to make this dogleg dado is to drill several stopped holes, then square the edges and corner with a chisel. (See Figures 1 and 2.)

1/To make the dogleg dadoes in the sides, first drill two or three ⅝"-diameter, ¼"-deep holes, removing most of the stock.

2/Then clean up the edges and the corner of the dogleg with a chisel.

5

Cut the shapes of the top, bottom, divider, and back. The back has a tongue at the top end from which to hang the clock by a peg or a hook, and the top and bottom are notched to fit around the back. The divider is notched to fit in the dogleg dadoes in the sides. Lay out the shapes of these parts as shown in the *Back Layout, Top Layout, Bottom Layout,* and *Divider Layout*. Cut the shapes with a band saw, scroll saw, or saber saw. Sand the sawed edges.

6

Make the cutouts in the sides and the back. Both sides have rectangular cutouts near the top ends. On the original clock case, these served as inspection windows through which the clockmaker could inspect the movement from time to time. The glass in them could be easily removed, allowing him to adjust or maintain the movement when needed. On this reproduction, however, the cutout in the back gives you access to the movement. The side cutouts are sound holes, letting you hear the chimes more clearly. They are covered with cloth instead of glass.

To make these cutouts, lay them out as shown in the *Side Layout* and *Back Layout*. Drill a hole about ½" in diameter through the waste in each part. Insert the blade of a saber saw or scroll saw through this hole and cut out the waste. File or sand the sawed edges. (See Figure 3.)

Note: If you are using a mechanical movement, you may want to change the size of the back cutout or eliminate it completely.

3/To make a cutout, first drill an access hole through the waste. This hole must be larger than the blade of your scroll saw or saber saw. Insert the blade through the hole and cut away the waste.

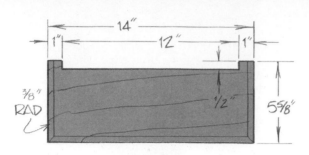

**TOP VIEW
BOTTOM LAYOUT**

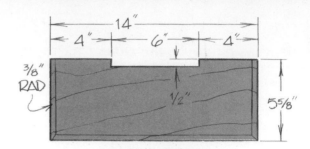

**BOTTOM VIEW
TOP LAYOUT**

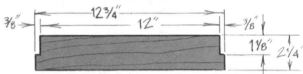

DIVIDER LAYOUT

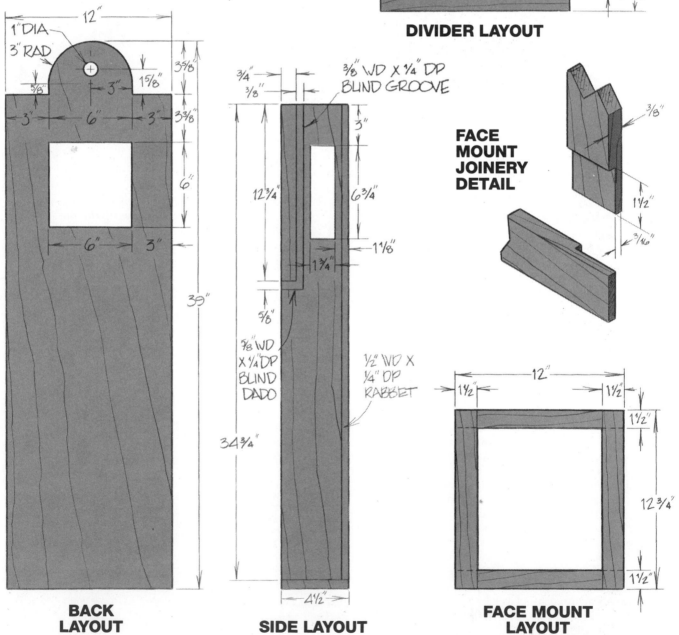

**FACE
MOUNT
JOINERY
DETAIL**

**BACK
LAYOUT**

SIDE LAYOUT

**FACE MOUNT
LAYOUT**

7

Round over the top, bottom, divider, and side cutouts. The front and side edges of the top and bottom are rounded over, as shown in the *Top/Bottom Profile*. So are the *inside* edges of the side cutouts. The front edge of the divider is rounded on the top and bottom, as shown in the *Divider Profile*.

Using a table-mounted router, round over the edges of the top, bottom, and side cutouts with a ³⁄₈″ quarter-round *piloted* bit. Switch to a ¹⁄₄″ quarter-round bit and round over the front edge of the divider.

Because the pilot of the router bit won't reach into the corners of the side cutouts, the shaped edge will make

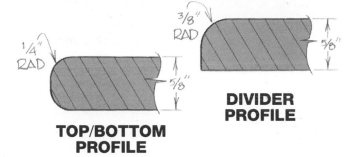

TOP/BOTTOM PROFILE

DIVIDER PROFILE

round corners. Square the corners with a carving chisel, making them appear as if they were mitered. (See Figures 4 and 5.)

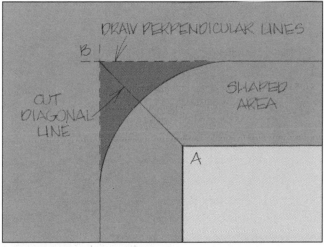

4/To square an inside corner of a routed shape, first cut a deep line with a carving chisel diagonally out from the corner (A). To determine how far this diagonal line should extend, imagine how the routed edges will look when they're squared off. Draw two perpendicular lines that define the extent of the shaped edges, then cut the diagonal line from the corner to where the perpendicular lines cross (B).

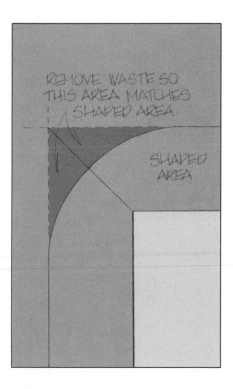

5/Carve away the waste on both sides of the diagonal line, following the profile of the router shape. When you're finished, the shape should look as if it were mitered and joined at the diagonal.

8

Cut the joinery for the face mount. The face mount rails and stiles are joined at the corners with lap joints. Cut the joints with a table-mounted router or dado cutter. (See Figure 6.)

6/When making lap joints, use a miter gauge to feed the stock over the cutter or bit. Make several passes to cut the entire length of the lap. Attach an extension and a stop block to the miter gauge to halt the cut automatically when the lap is long enough.

9

Drill or cut holes in the back and the speaker mount. Drill a 1″-diameter hole through the back, near the top end, as shown in the *Back Layout*. If you're making a speaker mount for the clock case, measure the diameter of the speaker. Using a hole saw, cut a hole through the center of the mount, making it ¼″ smaller than the speaker.

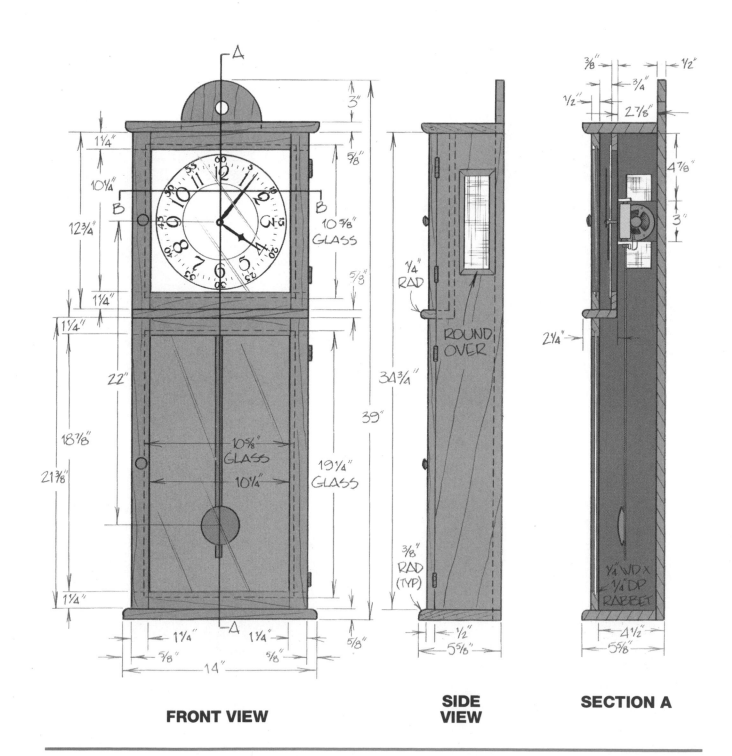

FRONT VIEW

SIDE VIEW

SECTION A

10

Assemble the clock case. Glue the face mount rails and stiles together, and make sure the assembly is perfectly square as you clamp it. Let the glue dry, then sand the joints clean and flush. Finish sand the parts and assembly you've made so far — back, top, bottom, divider, sides, and face mount.

Note: If you've purchased a hardboard face or have mounted a paper face to a hardboard backing, you may wish to rabbet the inside edges of the assembled face mount. Later, you can inset the face in this rabbet.

Glue together the sides, back, divider, and face mount. Let the glue dry, then glue the top and bottom to the sides. (Do *not* glue the top or bottom to the back.) Since the top and bottom are glued to the end grain of the sides, these glue joints won't be very strong. Reinforce the joints by driving cut nails through the top and bottom and into the sides. Also drive nails through the back and into the top and bottom. Set the nail heads,

but don't cover them with putty. This will imitate the look of old-time hand-forged nails.

Note: Cut nails sometimes act like tiny wedges, splitting the wood. To prevent this, drill pilot holes. These holes should be the same diameter as a nail shank measured halfway along its length.

> *TRY THIS!* Drive the nails at a slight angle to the right or left, alternating the direction with each nail. This will hook the parts together.

If you've made a speaker mount, glue it into place between the face mount and the back, as shown in *Section B*. Let the glue dry, then sand all joints clean and flush.

11

Cut the joinery in the door rails and stiles. The door parts are assembled with bridle joints — slot mortises and tenons. Make these

joints on a table saw, using either a dado cutter or an ordinary combination blade. (See Figures 7 and 8.) Cut the mortises in the stiles and the tenons in the rails.

7/To join the door parts, first cut a 1/4"-wide, 1 1/4"-deep slot mortise in each end of each stile. Use a tenoning jig to hold the stock vertical to the cutter.

8/Then cut a matching tenon in each end of each rail. Leave the height of the cutter where it is and adjust the position of the tenoning jig so the cutter saws a 1 1/4"-wide, 1/8"-deep rabbet in the face of the stock. Make one rabbet, then turn the stock around and make a second. The two rabbets will form a tenon.

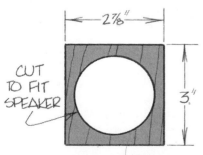

**SPEAKER MOUNT
LAYOUT**

CUT TO FIT SPEAKER

2 7/8"

3"

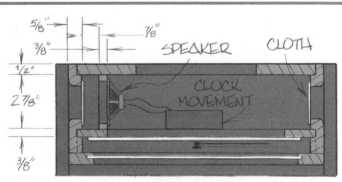

SECTION B

5/8"   7/8"   SPEAKER   CLOTH

3/8"

1/2"

2 7/8"

3/8"

CLOCK MOVEMENT

12 Assemble and fit the doors.
Dry assemble the door rails and stiles and fit them to the clock case. Plane or sand away a little stock from the edges of the rails and the ends of the stiles so the doors fit with a $\frac{1}{32}''$–$\frac{1}{16}''$ gap at the top and bottom.

Glue the door parts together and wipe away any excess glue with a wet rag. Before the glue dries, clamp the doors in place in the case, securing the door stiles to the sides of the case with bar clamps. This will ensure that the doors fit precisely after the glue sets.

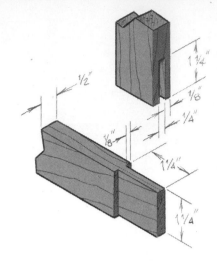

DOOR FRAME JOINERY DETAIL

13 Rabbet the doors to mount the glass.
Let the glue dry for *at least* 24 hours. Then clamp each door frame face down on your workbench. Rout a $\frac{1}{4}''$-wide, $\frac{1}{4}''$-deep rabbet on the back side, all around the inside edges, and square the corners with a chisel. (See Figure 9.) This rabbet will hold the glass in the door.

9/Cut the glass rabbet in the door rails and stiles **after** you've assembled the frames. Use a hand-held router and a piloted rabbeting bit.

14 Fit the doors and hardware to the case.
Mortise the right door stiles and the right side of the clock case for hinges, and mount the doors on the case. Install the door pulls on the left stiles. The position of these pulls isn't critical, but they should be approximately centered between the top and bottom of each stile.

Using small roundhead brass screws, attach the hooks to the left side of the case, even with the pulls. To give the hooks something to latch onto, install screws in the outside edge of the left stiles.

Attach the clock movement to the clock face (or the back of the clock case). If you have an external speaker, attach it to the speaker mount. Fasten the face to the face mount with small roundhead brass screws.

If necessary, trim the pendulum to the proper length. (On most electrical movements, the length of the pendulum does not affect the timekeeping — so you can make it any length.) Attach the pendulum and bob to the movement. Mount the hands on the hand shaft. Install a battery (or wind the movement) to check that the clock, chimes, and pendulum all work properly.

15 Finish the clock.
When you're satisfied that the clock operates properly, remove the hands, pendulum, face, movement, and speaker. Also remove the doors, hinges, and other hardware. Do any necessary touch-up sanding on the wood surfaces, then apply a finish to the clock case and door frames.

When the finish dries, install the glass in the doors, holding the panes in place with wire brads. Cut the cloth slightly larger than the cutouts in the sides. Paint the edges of the cloth with glue or varnish to prevent the weave from unraveling, then tack the cloth pieces to the inside of the case. Make sure the cloth covers the cutouts completely.

Reinstall the movement, speaker, and face. Mount the doors on the case, along with the pulls and hooks. Finally, attach the pendulum and bob to the movement.

TRY THIS! To make the completed clock look like an antique, you may want to tarnish the brass artificially — hinges, pulls, hooks, screws, pendulum, and bob. To do this, first soak the brass parts in lacquer thinner and wipe them clean. This removes the lacquer that most manufacturers apply to keep the brass bright.

Next, mix 2 tablespoons of salt in a cup of water to make a salt solution. Pour a coffee can one-third full of ammonia cleaner. Dip the brass parts in the salt water, then suspend them *above* the ammonia cleaner from a screen or string. Place the cover on the can and gently warm it with a heat gun. Do not make the can so hot that the ammonia boils. Inside, the brass will blacken. (You'll have to tarnish the long pendulum a few inches at a time, laying it across the top of the can and covering it with foil.) **Warning:** Do this tarnishing outdoors to avoid breathing the ammonia fumes.

When the brass is completely tarnished, dip it in salt water once more and let it dry overnight. Buff away *most* of the tarnish with #0000 steel wool, leaving the black in the cracks and around the edges.

Using Scrapers

It can sometimes take as long to sand and finish a project as it does to build it. However, you can reduce this time enormously by smoothing the wood with *cabinet scrapers* before you sand it. Scrapers are thin pieces of tool steel with a burr along one or more edges. When you push a scraper across the wood, the burr acts like a tiny plane iron, cutting a small amount of stock from the surface.

Scrapers level the wood much faster than sandpaper — a properly sharpened scraper will cut a smooth surface in a few passes. The only smoothing you should need to do after scraping a project is a light sanding with 150# (and finer) paper. Scrapers are also more economical than sandpaper, since you can use them over and over again. Yet most woodworkers don't take full advantage of their potential. Perhaps this is because a scraper doesn't stay sharp for long. The burr wears away quickly, and the "textbook" method for sharpening it is tedious and time-consuming. You have to wear away the old burr with a whetstone, file and hone the edge flat, then "roll" a new burr with a burnisher.

Most experienced woodworkers, however, will tell you that this complex sharpening procedure isn't necessary. You can put a fine edge on a scraper in a few seconds with a fine single-cut mill file.

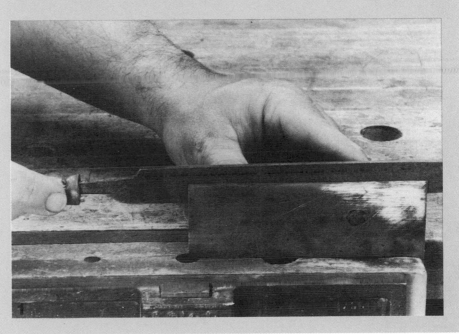

Clamp the dull scraper in a vice and remove the old burr with one or two strokes of the file. Keep the file flat against the face of the scraper and push forward quickly. File **both** faces, but don't remove too much metal. You don't want to make the scraper any thinner than it already is.

(Continued)

Using Scrapers — Continued

After filing the faces, file the edge of the scraper. Hold the file flat on the edge and tilt it about 2°–3° to the side on which you want to make the burr. Push forward slowly. Make several passes. This will create a burr on the edge.

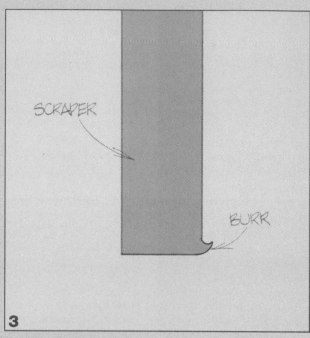

Test the scraper with your finger. You should be able to feel the burr on the edge where the file has rolled the metal.

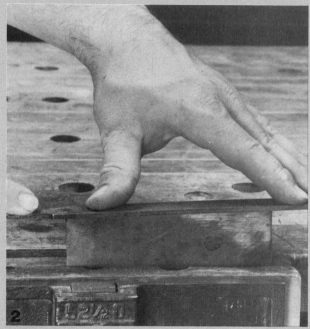

Hold the scraper in both hands with the burred edge flat on the wood. The burr should be facing away from you. Tilt the scraper forward slightly, then push it away from you, bearing down lightly on the wood. The burr should cut tiny curls, as if you were using a block plane with the iron adjusted to make **very** light cuts.

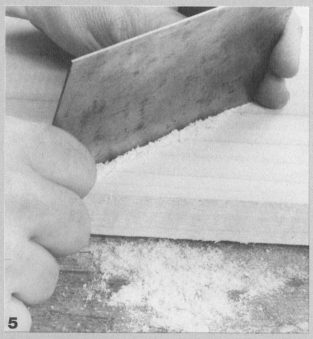

After using the scraper for 10–30 minutes (depending on the hardness of the wood), it will throw fewer and fewer curls and begin making sawdust. This means the burr is worn and dull. Take a few seconds to sharpen it again, then resume smoothing the wood.

Nesting Doves Peg Rack

The simple peg is one of the most versatile storage devices ever invented. For centuries, folks have used them to hang clothes, cooking utensils, even small pieces of furniture — almost anything that could be lifted off the floor.

The pegs are usually driven into a long board, called a pegboard, so they can be easily attached to a wall. The assembled pegs and pegboard create a "rack" of pegs — or peg rack, as it came to be called. Occasionally, old-time makers decorated their peg racks with painted patterns and simple carvings. The nesting doves are one such design. ●

Materials List

FINISHED DIMENSIONS

PARTS

Small Peg Rack

A. Pegboard   ½″ x 3½″ x 16½″
B. Pegs (5)   ½″ dia. x 1¾″
C. Dowels (2)   ¼″ dia. x ¾″
D. Beads (2)   ½″ dia.

Large Peg Rack

A. Pegboard   ¾″ x 7″ x 33″
B. Pegs (5)   ⅞″ dia. x 3½″
C. Dowels (2)   ¼″ dia. x 1″
D. Beads (2)   ¾″ dia.

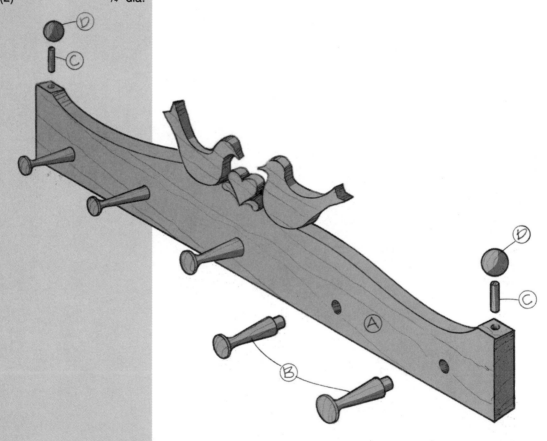

HARDWARE

Small Peg Rack
¼″ Molly anchors (2)

Large Peg Rack
⅜″ Molly anchors (2)

EXPLODED VIEW

1 Decide what size to make the peg rack.

Depending on what you have to hang, you can make the peg rack large or small. The small rack will hold mugs, hand towels, cooking utensils, and similar small items. The large rack is better suited for coats, clothes, umbrellas, and so on.

2 Select the stock and cut it to size.

Whether you're building the large or the small peg rack, you can make the pegboard from scrap lumber as long as the grain is straight and free of defects. Select a moderately soft, easy-to-carve wood, such as white pine or mahogany. The pegboards shown are made from pine.

Purchase the pegs and beads from a hobby store or woodworking supply company. Commercial pegs and beads are usually made from a hardwood such as birch or maple. If you would rather turn them yourself, you can make them from any clear wood you have on hand.

When you have selected the wood, plane and cut it to the sizes shown in the Materials List.

3 Drill holes in the pegboard and beads.

Make three sets of holes in the pegboard, as shown in the *Front View* and *Side View*. While you're at it, also drill holes in the wooden beads. (See Figure 1.) Here's a list for the small pegboard:

- Five $1/4''$-diameter, $1/4''$-deep holes in the face of the pegboard to hold the pegs
- Two $1/4''$-diameter, $3/8''$-deep holes in the upper edge of the pegboard to mount the beads
- A $1/4''$-diameter, $3/8''$-deep hole in each wooden bead to mount it to the pegboard
- Two $3/16''$-diameter holes through the pegboard, near the upper corners, to mount it to the wall

Here's a list for the large pegboard:

- Five $1/2''$-diameter, $5/8''$-deep holes in the face of the pegboard to hold the pegs
- Two $1/4''$-diameter, $1/2''$-deep holes in the upper edge of the pegboard to mount the beads

1/To keep a wooden bead from rolling around when you drill it, first drill a hole, slightly smaller than the diameter of the bead, through a scrap of wood. Rest the bead in the hole, then drill the bead.

- A $1/4''$-diameter, $1/2''$-deep hole in each wooden bead to mount it to the pegboard
- Two $3/16''$-diameter holes through the pegboard, near the upper corners, to mount it to the wall

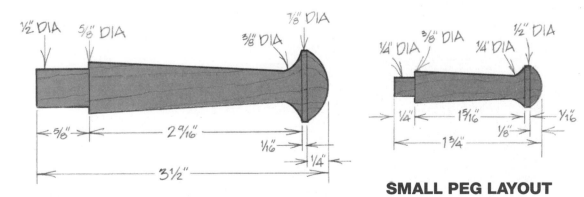

LARGE PEG LAYOUT

SMALL PEG LAYOUT

4 *Cut the shape of the pegboard.* Enlarge
the pattern for the pegboard. Trace it onto the
stock, then cut the shape with a saber saw, band saw,
or scroll saw. Sand the sawed edges to remove the saw
marks.

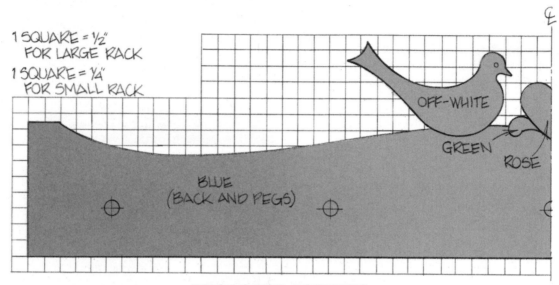

PEGBOARD PATTERN

1 SQUARE = ½"
FOR LARGE RACK
1 SQUARE = ¼"
FOR SMALL RACK

BLUE
(BACK AND PEGS)

OFF-WHITE

GREEN

ROSE

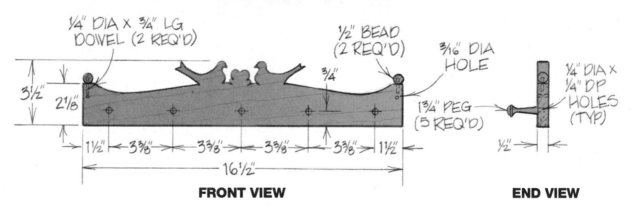

FRONT VIEW   **END VIEW**

LARGE PEG RACK

¼" DIA X ¾" LG
DOWEL (2 REQ'D)

½" BEAD
(2 REQ'D)

³⁄₁₆ DIA
HOLE

¼" DIA X
¼" DP
HOLES
(TYP)

1¾" PEG
(5 REQ'D)

3½"
2⅛"
¾"
1½"   3⅜"   3⅜"   3⅜"   3⅜"   1½"
16½"
½"

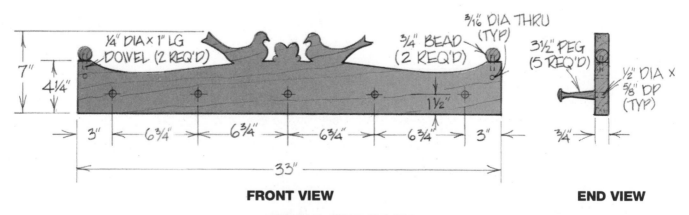

FRONT VIEW   **END VIEW**

SMALL PEG RACK

¼" DIA X 1" LG
DOWEL (2 REQ'D)

³⁄₁₆ DIA THRU
(TYP)

¾" BEAD
(2 REQ'D)

3½" PEG
(5 REQ'D)

½" DIA X
⅝" DP
(TYP)

7"
4¼"
1½"
3"   6¾"   6¾"   6¾"   6¾"   3"
33"
¾"

5 **Carve the pegboard.** To emphasize the shapes of the doves and heart, carve grooves around them. You may also rout these grooves with a point-cut quarter-round bit. Don't cut the grooves too deep. They should be just deep enough to make the elements of the design stand out from one another. (See Figure 2.) Round over the edges of the doves and heart with a file and sandpaper.

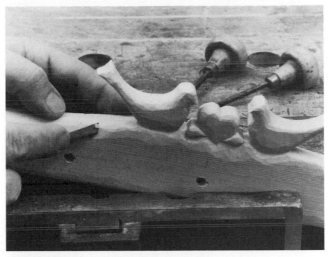

2/Carve or rout shallow grooves around the dove and the heart to make the shapes stand out from one another. Then round over the edges of the shapes.

6 **Assemble the peg rack.** Finish sand all the wooden parts, and slightly round the ends and edges of the pegboard. Spread glue evenly on the peg tenons and inside the mounting holes in the pegboard. Press the pegs into the holes.

Apply glue all along the length of the dowels, and put glue in the holes in both the wooden beads and the upper corners of the pegboard. Press the dowels into the pegboard, then mount the beads on the dowels. Wipe away any excess glue with a wet rag.

7 **Paint the peg rack.** Do any necessary touch-up sanding. Then paint the peg rack with the colors shown in the *Pegboard Pattern* or use a color scheme of your own.

8 **Hang the peg rack.** Position the rack on the wall where you want to hang it. With a pencil, mark the locations of the two mounting holes on the wall. Drill ¼"-diameter holes (for the small peg rack) or ⅜"-diameter holes (for the large peg rack) through the wall and insert Molly anchors in the holes. Set the Mollies by tightening the bolts. Back the bolts out of the Mollies, insert them through the mounting holes in the pegboard, and secure the rack to the Molly anchors. (See Figure 3.)

Note: Molly anchors will work for *most* (but not all) situations. If one or more of the peg rack mounting holes is positioned over a wall stud, use a #10 x 3" roundhead wood screw in each hole to mount the rack. If the wall is masonry, use expandable lead shields and lag screws instead of Mollies or wood screws.

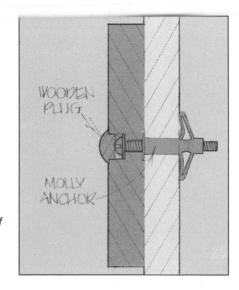

3/When you set a Molly anchor, it expands inside the wall, fastening itself permanently in place. You can then bolt the peg rack to the anchor.

Accent Table

A small, low table has dozens of uses. It's a good display stand for collectibles, plants, a portable television, photo albums, and other items. It can be a catchall for magazines, knitting, or hobby work. You can use a small table as a TV tray, side table, or game table. It even makes a good footrest.

A table such as this is also extremely easy to build. Because it's too small to hold anything heavy, you needn't join the legs to the aprons with mortises and tenons. Simple dowel joints will be strong enough, in most cases. This helps reduce the time and effort it takes to build the table.

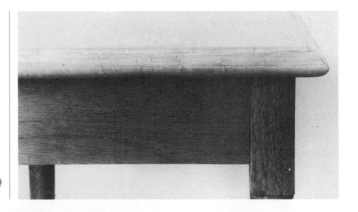

Materials List

FINISHED DIMENSIONS

PARTS

A. Top $3/4'' \times 14^{1}/2'' \times 21^{1}/4''$

B. Legs (4) $1^{1}/2'' \times 1^{1}/2'' \times 19^{3}/4''$

C. Front aprons (2) $3/4'' \times 3'' \times 16^{1}/4''$

D. Side aprons (2) $3/4'' \times 3'' \times 9^{1}/2''$

E. Dowels (16) $3/8''$ dia. $\times 2''$

F. Clips (6) $5/8'' \times 1^{1}/2'' \times 1^{1}/2''$

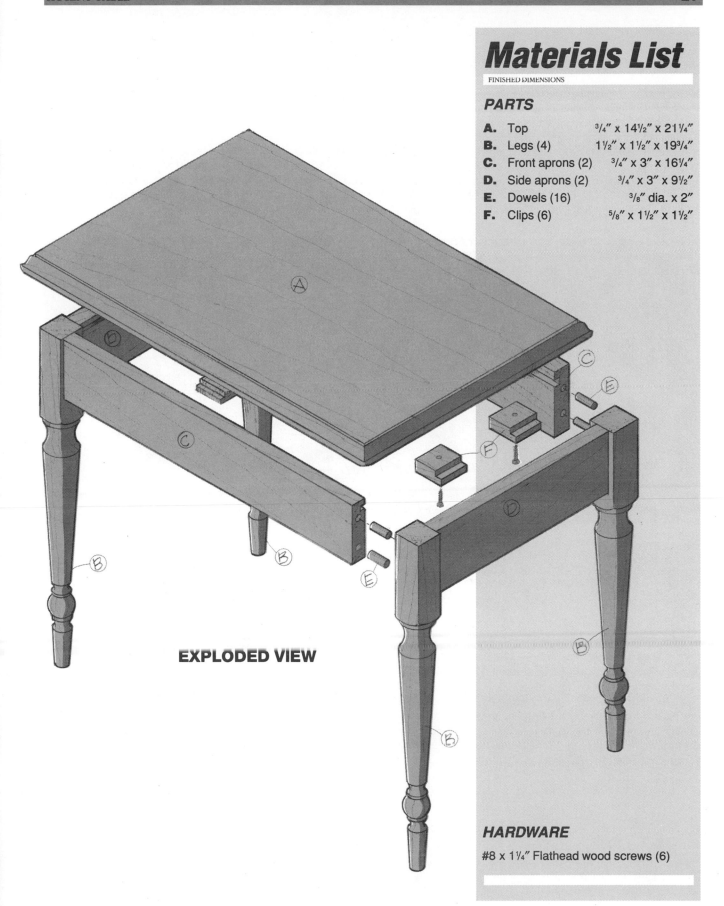

EXPLODED VIEW

HARDWARE

#8 x $1^{1}/4''$ Flathead wood screws (6)

1

Select the stock and cut it to size. To make this project, you need approximately 5 board feet of 4/4 (four-quarters) lumber, and 3 board feet of 8/4 (eight-quarters) lumber. You can use most kinds of cabinet-grade hardwood or softwood, although harder woods will wear longer. The accent table shown is made from bird's-eye maple and mahogany.

Plane the 4/4 stock to ³/₄″ thick. Rip a 1¹/₂″-wide, 12″ long piece from a ³/₄″-thick board, and plane this to ⁵/₈″ thick. Cut the clips from the ⁵/₈″-thick stock. Glue up the stock for the top from ³/₄″-thick lumber, and cut it to size. Cut the aprons from the remaining ³/₄″-thick wood.

Plane one face of the 8/4 stock smooth, then joint one edge so it's exactly 90° from the smooth face. Rip 1³/₄″-wide leg blanks from the stock, and joint *one* edge of each blank. Once again, the jointed edges should be exactly 90° from the planed faces. Plane each leg blank to 1¹/₂″ square, removing material from the rough face and the unjointed edge *only*. (See Figures 1 through 3.)

Cut the leg blanks and the dowels to length.

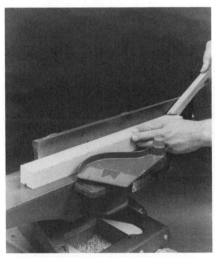

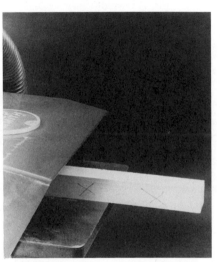

1/To make a perfectly square leg blank, first joint the stock so you have two smooth surfaces exactly 90° from each other.

2/Mark the smooth surfaces with a pencil.

3/Plane the blank to the required dimensions, removing stock from the rough surfaces **only**. Do **not** remove the pencil marks. When you finish, all four surfaces should be square to one another.

2

Join the aprons and the legs with dowels. Drill ³/₈″-diameter, 1″ deep holes for dowels in the ends of the aprons. Use a doweling jig to guide the drill, making two holes in each end of each board, as shown in the *Front View* and *Side View*. Use dowel centers to locate matching holes in the legs, then drill them. (See Figure 4.) Dry assemble the legs and the aprons to check the fit of the dowel joints.

4/After drilling dowel holes in the aprons, mark the legs to make matching holes. To locate these holes, insert dowel centers in the ends of each apron. Measure and mark the locations of the aprons on the legs. Then press the end of each apron against its leg. The dowel centers will leave small indentations, showing where to drill the holes.

3 *Turn or cut the shapes of the legs.*

Unless you've chosen an *Alternate Leg Design*, turn the legs on a lathe. Try to match them as closely as possible. To do this, first make a *storystick* following the dimensions on the *Leg Layout*. Use this storystick to mark each leg blank after you've rounded it, but before you turn the shapes. As you turn, carefully measure the diameters of the shapes with calipers so they will all be the same on each leg. (See Figures 5 through 9.) Finish sand the legs on the lathe.

5/To make duplicate turnings, first make a **storystick** that shows the profile of the turning as well as the diameters of all the beads, coves, flats, and tapers. After rounding the stock, use this storystick to mark the positions of the shapes on the spindle.

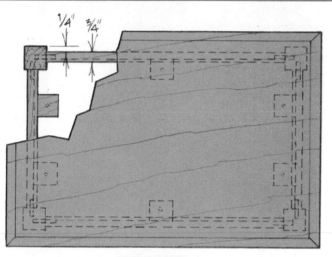

TOP VIEW

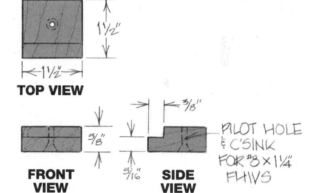

TOP VIEW

FRONT VIEW   SIDE VIEW

PILOT HOLE & C'SINK FOR #8 × 1¼" FHWS

CLIP LAYOUT

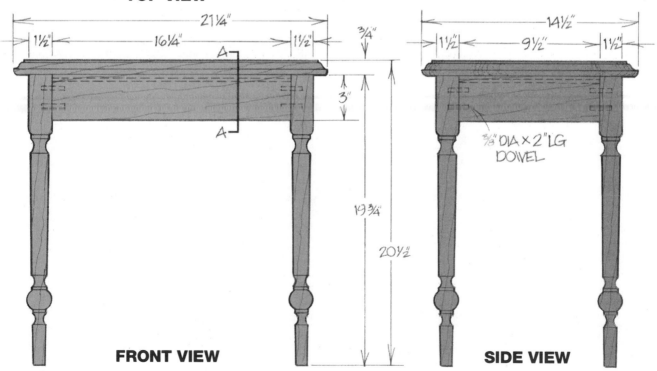

FRONT VIEW

SIDE VIEW

³⁄₈" DIA × 2" LG DOWEL

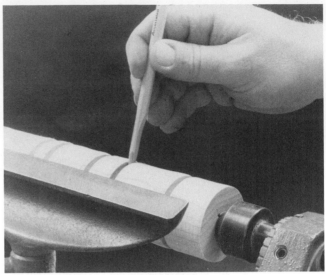

6/When you have marked the spindle, turn the diameters of the various shapes with a parting tool. Set the calipers to each diameter before you turn it. Hold the calipers in one hand and the parting tool in the other, letting the calipers rest in the groove created by the parting tool. As soon as the calipers slip over the spindle, stop cutting. Repeat for each diameter.

7/These grooves are the starting and stopping points for each shape. If you turn to the bottoms of these grooves — and no further — the diameters of the various shapes will match from turning to turning. To make sure that you don't cut too deeply, shade the bottoms of the grooves with a pencil.

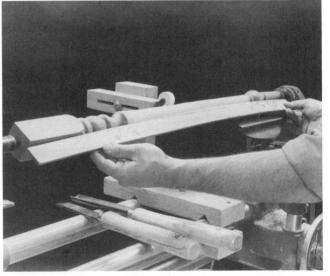

8/Turn the beads, coves, and other shapes. As you work, be careful not to remove the pencil marks at the bottoms of the grooves.

9/As the spindle takes shape on the lathe, check your progress now and then with the story-stick. Compare the shapes on the profile with those in the turning, and try to match them as closely as possible. By using the story-stick as a guide and following this procedure for each spindle, you can match the spindles almost exactly.

If you wish to turn or cut some other leg shape besides the one shown in the *Leg Layout,* the *Alternate Leg Designs* show two possible leg shapes that you may use instead. To make the Hepplewhite design, taper the two *inside* surfaces. Cut these tapers on a table saw, using a tapering jig. To make the Chippendale design, cut three $3/16$"-diameter beads in the two *outside* surfaces of each leg, using a router, shaper, or molder.

4

Cut the grooves in the aprons. As shown in *Section A,* the top is "clipped" to the aprons. The ends of these clips fit in ³⁄₈"-wide, ³⁄₈"-deep grooves in the inside surfaces of the aprons. Cut these grooves with a router or dado cutter.

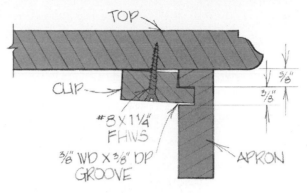

SECTION A

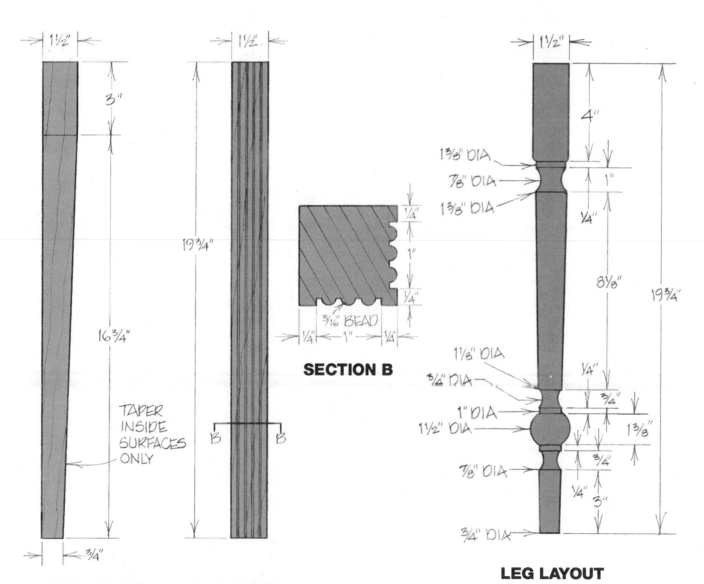

SECTION B

LEG LAYOUT

HEPPLEWHITE
(SQUARE TAPER)

CHIPPENDALE
(STRAIGHT WITH BEADING)

ALTERNATE LEG DESIGNS

5 Cut the rabbets in the clips.

Cut the rabbets in the clips. Using a table-mounted router or a dado cutter, cut a ³/₈″-wide, ⁵/₁₆″-deep rabbet in one end of each clip (*across the grain*). To control the small parts safely, feed them into the bit or cutter with a miter gauge and miter gauge extension. (See Figure 10.)

10/To safely cut the rabbets in the clips, use a miter gauge and an extension to feed the clips across the cutter. Clamp an L-shaped stop block to the extension to position each clip and keep it from rising up as it's cut.

6 Shape the edges and ends of the top.

Shape the edges and ends of the top. The top edges and ends are shaped so the top will appear thinner and more delicate than it really is. Cut this shape with a router or shaper, duplicating the *Top Edge Profile* or creating a profile of your own design.

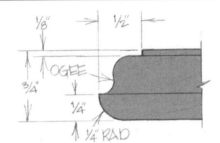

TOP EDGE PROFILE

7 Assemble the table.

Assemble the table. Finish sand the top and aprons. Assemble the legs and aprons with dowels and glue. Let the glue dry, then turn the leg assembly upside down on the top and clamp it in position. Put the clips in place with the rabbeted ends in the apron grooves. Drill a pilot hole through the center of each clip, then secure the clip to the top with a flathead wood screw. Tighten the screw so the clip is snug, but not too tight. The tabletop must be able to expand and contract with changes in humidity.

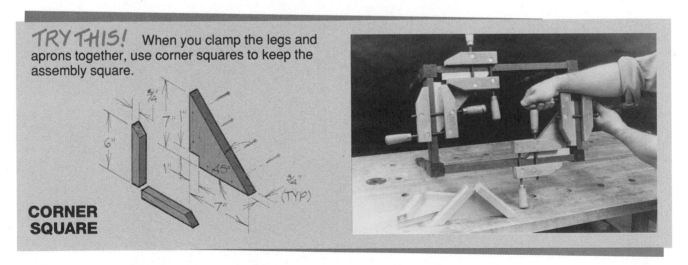

TRY THIS! When you clamp the legs and aprons together, use corner squares to keep the assembly square.

CORNER SQUARE

8 Finish the table.

Finish the table. Mark the position of each clip, then disassemble the top from the leg assembly. Do any necessary touch-up sanding — but be careful not to sand off the marks that show you which clip goes where! Apply a finish to the completed table, covering all surfaces — inside and out, top and bottom. Let the finish dry and replace the top on the table, securing it with the clips.

Recycling Bins

While recycling makes good sense, it presents a storage problem for most homeowners. Recycling centers demand that you separate your trash into at least four categories — paper, plastic, metal, and glass. Some centers ask that you further separate the types of metal, colors of glass, and so on. This requires you to have at least one container for each type of trash, and yet most kitchens only have room for a single trash can.

These recycling bins solve this problem. There are four large bins to hold different types of trash, plus a shelf for newspaper. Still, the entire unit takes up no more floor space than an ordinary 20-gallon kitchen garbage pail.

In addition to being space efficient, this project is also easy to use. Each bin is designed to be easily filled *and* easily emptied. The bins are all open to the front and to the sides for convenient access. When a bin fills up, simply release a latch, fold down the bin front, and scrape the contents into a bag or larger container.

Materials List

FINISHED DIMENSIONS

PARTS

A. Sides (2) $3/4'' \times 11^3/4'' \times 47^1/4''$

B. Shelves (5) $3/4'' \times 11^1/2'' \times 15^1/4''$

C. Top $3/4'' \times 12^1/2'' \times 17^1/2''$

D. Back* $1/4'' \times 15^1/4'' \times 44^7/8''$

E. Top/top middle
doors (2) $3/4'' \times 3^1/2'' \times 16''$

F. Bottom middle
door $3/4'' \times 4^1/2'' \times 16''$

G. Bottom door $3/4'' \times 5^1/2'' \times 16''$

H. Toeboard $3/4'' \times 2^3/4'' \times 16''$

Make this part from plywood.

HARDWARE

#10 x 1¼" Flathead wood screws
  (42–48)

4d Finishing nails (18–24)

1½" x 2" Butt hinges and mounting
  screws (8)

Small hooks and eyes (8)

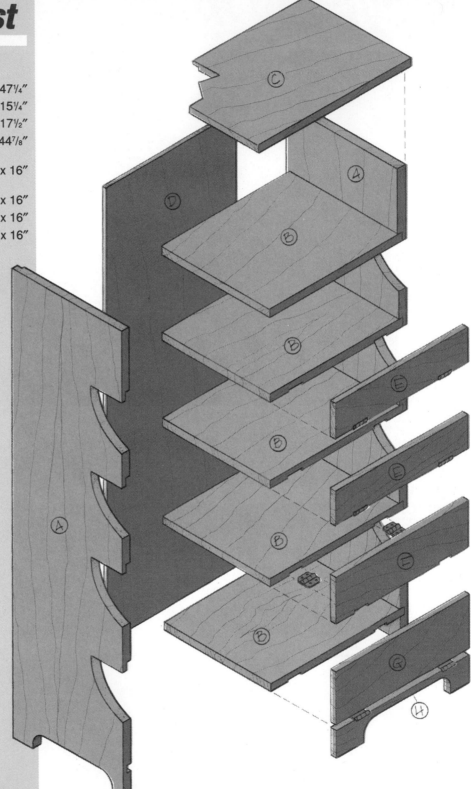

EXPLODED VIEW

1

Select the stock and cut it to size. To make this project, you need about 20 board feet of 4/4 (four-quarters) lumber and a 4' x 4' sheet of ¼" plywood. Use an inexpensive, close-grain wood that wears well and won't absorb moisture readily. The bins shown are made from poplar, but you might also use maple or birch. You can also use birch plywood, if you face the ends.

Plane the 4/4 stock to ¾" thick. If necessary, glue up the stock needed for the wide parts — sides, shelves, and top. Then cut all the parts to the sizes shown in the Materials List.

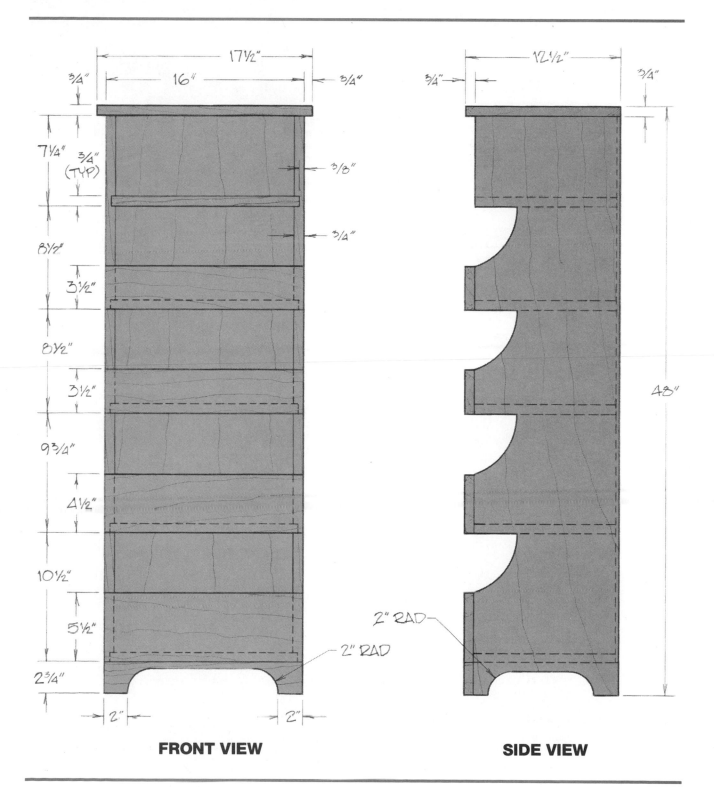

FRONT VIEW

SIDE VIEW

2

Cut the dadoes and rabbets in the sides and top. The shelves rest in ³/₄″-wide, ³/₈″-deep dadoes in the sides, and the top fits in ¹/₄″-wide, ³/₈″-deep rabbets in the sides and the top. Lay out the dadoes and rabbets on the stock as shown in the *Side Layout* and *Top Layout/Bottom View*. Cut these joints with a router or a dado cutter. Note that the top rabbet is *double-blind* — closed at both ends. Square the closed ends with a hand chisel. (See Figures 1 and 2.)

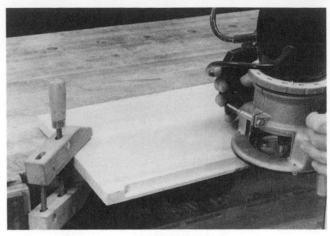

1/When routing blind joints, the easiest tool to use is a hand-held router. It allows you to see where you should start and stop cutting. Mark the joints clearly on the wood and keep the sawdust cleared away as you cut.

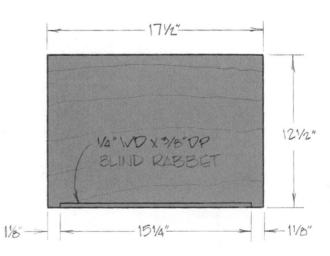

2/If necessary, square the blind ends of a routed joint with a hand chisel. You may use a corner chisel, if you have one.

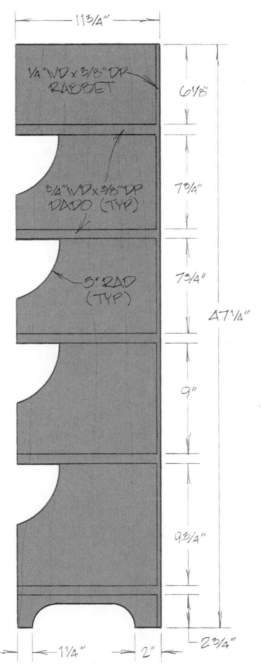

11¾″

¼″WD x ³/₈″DP RABBET

6⅛″

³/₄″WD x ³/₈″DP DADO (TYP)

7¾″

5″RAD (TYP)

7¾″

47¼″

9″

9¾″

1¼″   2″

2¾″

SIDE LAYOUT

17½″

¼″WD x ³/₈″DP BLIND RABBET

12½″

1⅛″   15¼″   1⅛″

TOP LAYOUT/BOTTOM VIEW

3

Cut the shapes of the sides and toe-board. The sides of the bins are relieved, or scalloped, so you can access them from three directions. Lay out the scallops on *one* side, as shown in the *Scallop Detail*. Also lay out the shape of the feet on the toeboard and the same side that you marked for the scallops. Stack the marked side on top of the other side, taking care that the ends and edges are flush and that the dadoes line up. Temporarily nail the boards together with finishing nails.

Cut the shape of the sides and the toeboard with a saber saw or coping saw. (See Figure 3.) Sand the sawed edges, then remove the nails from the sides. The sides will be mirror images of each other.

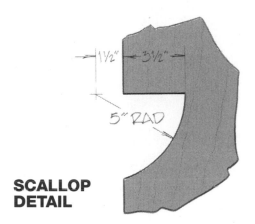

SCALLOP DETAIL

3/To save time, tack the sides together with finishing nails and cut the scallops in both parts at once.

4

Assemble the bins. Finish sand all the parts. Glue the shelves to the sides, using a waterproof glue such as epoxy or resorcinol. Reinforce the glue joints with flathead wood screws, driving the screws through the sides and into the ends of the shelves. Counterbore *and* countersink these screws, then cover the heads with wooden plugs. Sand the plugs flush with the surface of the wood.

Glue the top to the sides, lining up the blind ends of the top rabbet with the rabbets in the sides. The back edge of the top should be flush with the back of the bin

assembly, and it should overhang the bins ³/₄″ on the other three sides. Reinforce the top with wood screws, and cover the heads with wooden plugs.

Fit the plywood back to the top and side rabbets, and secure it with finishing nails. Do *not* glue the back in place. Depending on the sorts of things you throw in the bins, the plywood back may be exposed to lots of moisture. Eventually, the plies will delaminate and you'll need to replace the back. If the back is just nailed in place, it will be easy to remove.

5

Attach the doors to the bins. The fronts of the bins all swing down to make them easier to empty. Mortise the lower edge of the bottom door and the top edge of the toeboard for hinges. (The other

three doors don't need to be mortised.) Mount the doors to the bins. Install small hooks and eyes, one near each end of each door, to hold the doors closed.

6

Finish the bins. Remove the doors and all the hardware from the completed bins. Do any necessary touch-up sanding, then apply a finish to all

wooden surfaces. Use a washable, waterproof finish, such as polyurethane or exterior paint. When the finish dries, reassemble the bins and doors.

Turkey Whirligig

Wind-powered toys have been around for hundreds — perhaps thousands — of years. You can find examples of them in all areas of the globe. However, nowhere have they been more popular than in America. When we were a young nation, parents built special "Sunday toys" for their children to encourage quiet, reflective play during the Sabbath. Some were powered by natural forces — wind, water, or gravity — while the children watched. Wind-powered Sunday toys were nicknamed "whirligigs."

This turkey whirligig is typical of old-time Sunday toys. When the wind blows, the weathercock turns the turkey so it faces the wind. The tail spins, flashing its colors. When the wind shifts, the turkey turns and the tail continues to whirl. Only a light breeze is needed to set it spinning, so the whirligig will work in a variety of locations, both indoors and out — in a garden, on a porch, even in front of an open window.

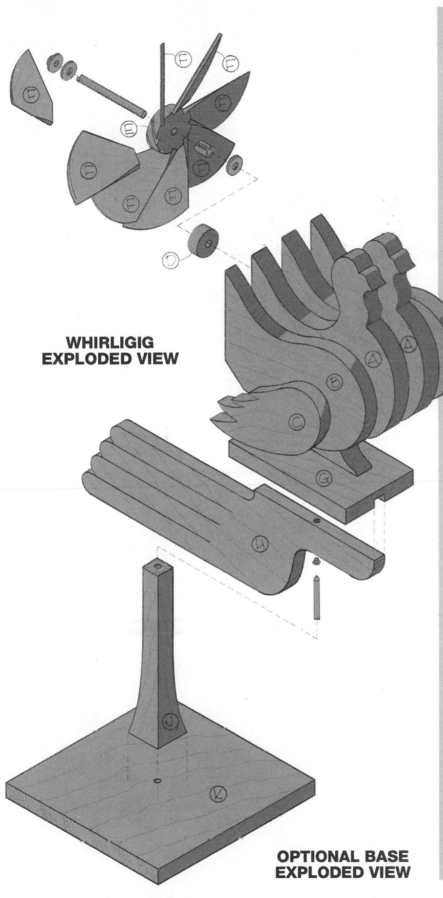

**WHIRLIGIG
EXPLODED VIEW**

**OPTIONAL BASE
EXPLODED VIEW**

Materials List

FINISHED DIMENSIONS

PARTS

A.	Body (2)	³/₄″ x 7¹/₄″ x 10³/₄″
B.	Right/left side (2)	¹/₂″ x 6³/₄″ x 7¹/₄″
C.	Wings (2)	¹/₂″ x 3¹/₄″ x 6⁵/₈″
D.	Spacer	1″ dia. x ³/₄″
E.	Hub	2¹/₂″ dia. x ³/₄″
F.	Wind vanes (8)	¹/₈″ x 4³/₄″ x 5″
G.	Platform	³/₄″ x 3¹/₂″ x 6″
H.	Weathercock	¹/₂″ x 5″ x 15″
J.	Post (optional)	1³/₄″ x 1³/₄″ x 8³/₄″
K.	Base (optional)	³/₄″ x 9³/₄″ x 9³/₄″

HARDWARE

#8 x 1¹/₄″ Flathead wood screws (2)
#10 x 2¹/₂″ Flathead wood screws (2
  or 3)
10d Nail
³/₁₆″ dia. x 3³/₈″ Steel rod
¹/₄″ dia. x 3¹/₂″ *or* 7″ Steel rod
⁵/₁₆″ O.D. x ³/₄″ Roll pin
#12 Flat washers (2)
³/₁₆″ Push nut

1 **Select the stock and cut it to size.** To build this project, you need approximately 4 board feet of 4/4 (four-quarters) lumber, a 2′ x 2′ sheet of ⅛″ plywood, and a scrap of 1″-diameter dowel. If you want to make the optional stand, you'll also need a scrap of 8/4 (eight-quarters) lumber. Most of the parts are small enough that you can make them from scraps. Since you're going to paint the completed project anyway, it won't matter if you mix different types of wood. The turkey whirligig shown is made from three different types of scrap wood.

However, if you're going to use this project outdoors, you should give more thought to the materials.

Mahogany, cedar, redwood, and cypress all weather better than other wood species. Don't use ordinary plywood for the wind vanes; it will delaminate after a few rain storms. Instead, make your own plywood from a weather-resistant wood. Using waterproof epoxy, glue two pieces of ⅛″-thick stock together with the grains perpendicular. Let the epoxy dry, then plane ¹⁄₁₆″ from each side. The laminated stock should be ⅛″ thick.

When you've selected and prepared the lumber, plane the solid wood to the thicknesses needed. Cut the platform, spacer, post, and base to size, and cut the remaining parts about ¼″ wider and longer than specified.

2 **Cut the shapes needed.** Enlarge the *Turkey Pattern, Wind Vane Pattern,* and *Weathercock Pattern.* Make one copy each of the *Wind Vane Pattern* and *Weathercock Pattern,* and five copies of the *Turkey Pattern.* With a scissors, cut up four of the turkey patterns so you have a right middle, left middle, side, and wing pattern. (These shapes are shown in the small drawings above the *Turkey Pattern.*) Keep the fifth turkey pattern whole; you'll need it later.

Stack the two wing pieces face to face, sticking them together with double-faced carpet tape. Do the same for the side pieces. Stack all eight of the wind vane pieces. Using spray adhesive, stick the patterns — right middle, left middle, side, wing, wind vane, and weathercock — to the appropriate stock. Also, scribe a 2½″-diameter circle on the hub stock.

TRY THIS! Because of the large number of interior lines in the *Turkey Pattern,* use either a pantograph, an opaque projector, or an enlarging/reducing photocopier to enlarge the pattern. The easiest method is to use a photocopier. Many "quick-print" companies have these — call around until you find one with a *variable* enlarging and reducing capability. This will allow you to enlarge the pattern to the exact size needed.

Cut all the shapes in each stack with a band saw or a scroll saw. Also cut the right middle and left middle. Sand the sawed edges, take the stacks apart, and discard the tape.

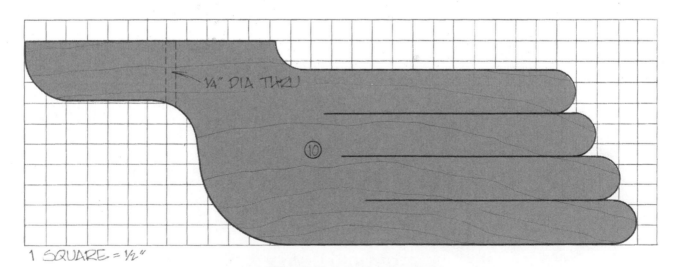

WEATHERCOCK PATTERN

3

Cut a groove in the platform. The weathercock fits in a ½"-wide, ³/8"-deep groove in the platform, as shown in the *Front View*. Cut this groove with a dado cutter or table-mounted router.

RIGHT MIDDLE
(CUT ONE)

LEFT MIDDLE
(CUT ONE)

RIGHT/LEFT SIDE
(CUT TWO)

RIGHT/LEFT WING
(CUT TWO)

COLOR CHART

1. BLACK
2. ANTIQUE WHITE
3. RED
4. VIOLET
5. DARK BROWN
6. BRICK
7. RUST
8. DARK RUST
9. LIGHT RUST
10. BASE: GREEN
11. TWO BLADES EACH:
    - (A) PURPLE
    - (B) RED
    - (C) TURQUOISE
    - (D) GREEN

1 SQUARE = ½"

TURKEY PATTERN

3/16" DIA x 1½" DP HOLE

SIDE

WING

LEFT MIDDLE

RIGHT MIDDLE

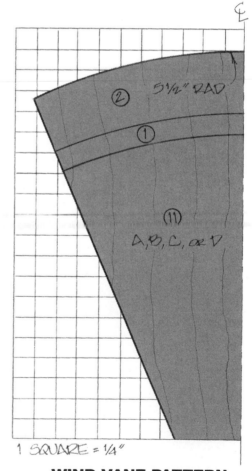

1 SQUARE = ¼"

WIND VANE PATTERN

5½" RAD

A, B, C, or D

4 Cut the grooves in the hub.

Cut the grooves in the hub. The wind vanes rest in eight ⅛"-wide, ½"-deep grooves around the circumference of the hub. These grooves are cut at a 30° angle to the face of the hub, as shown in the *Hub Layout*. The angled grooves cant the vanes into the wind and cause the tail to spin.

Make the grooves on a table saw, using a blade that cuts a ⅛"-wide kerf. Divide the hub into eighths, marking the circumference every 45°. Also, drill a 5/16"-diameter hole through the center of the hub.

To help cut the grooves, attach an extension to the miter gauge, as shown in the *Miter Gauge Extension Layout,* and adjust the angle of the gauge to 30°. Set the blade ½" above the table. Turn the saw on and push the miter gauge forward, cutting an angled kerf in the extension. Remove the extension from the gauge and drill a 5/16"-diameter hole through it. The center of this hole must be ⅝" to one side of the kerf, between the kerf and the miter gauge mounting holes. Draw an index mark about 1¼" above the hole.

Replace the extension on the miter gauge. Using a 5/16" carriage bolt, flat washer, and wing nut, secure the hub to the extension, in front of the kerf. Turn the hub, aligning one of the marks on the circumference with the index mark on the extension. Tighten the wing nut.

Turn the table saw on and push the miter gauge forward, cutting a groove in the edge of the hub. Turn the saw off and let it come to a stop. Pull the gauge back,

loosen the wing nut, and turn the hub one-eighth revolution so the next circumference mark lines up with the index mark. Tighten the nut, turn the saw on, and cut another groove. Repeat, cutting all eight grooves. (See Figure 1.) Remove the hub from the extension.

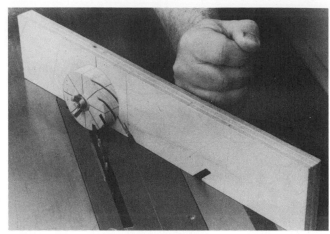

1/To cut the grooves in the edge of the hub, mount the hub on a miter gauge extension. Angle the extension, then feed the extension and the hub across the blade. To make sure these grooves are evenly spaced, mark the circumference of the hub every 45°. Line up a circumference mark with an index mark on the extension before cutting each groove.

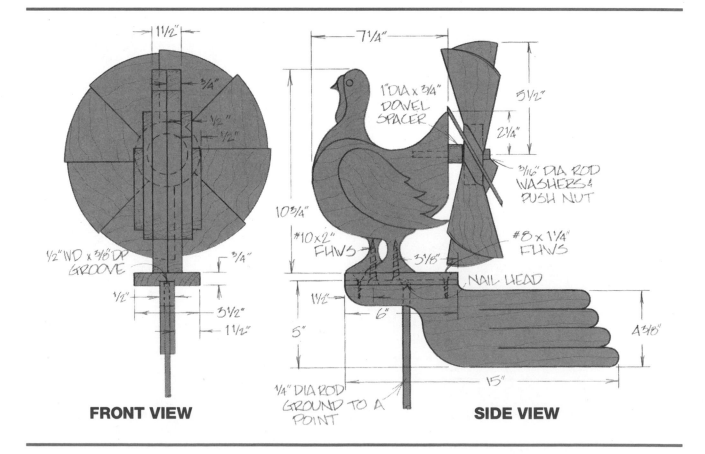

FRONT VIEW **SIDE VIEW**

½"WD x ⅜"DP GROOVE

1½" ¾" ½" ½"

¾" ½" 3½" 1½"

7¼" 5½" 2¼"

1"DIA x ¾" DOWEL SPACER

3/16" DIA ROD WASHERS & PUSH NUT

#8 x 1¼" FHWS

NAIL HEAD

10¾" #10x2" FHWS 3⅛"

1½" 6" 5" A⅜"

15"

¼" DIA ROD GROUND TO A POINT

5

Assemble and shape the turkey. Glue the right middle, left middle, and sides together, wiping away the excess glue with a wet rag. Let the glue dry, then sand the edges flush. Place the remaining turkey pattern over the turkey body. With an awl, show where to position the wing by poking several pinholes through the pattern and into a side. Turn the turkey over and repeat for the other wing. Glue the wings to the body.

Note: If you plan to display this project outside, use waterproof epoxy or resorcinol glue for assembly.

Using a doweling jig, drill a ³/₁₆″-diameter, 1½″-deep hole in the tail of the turkey. (See Figure 2.) Then round the edges of the turkey parts to give the turkey a more realistic shape. (See Figure 3.) If you wish, carve the beak, gobbler, and other details on the turkey.

TRY THIS! To keep glued-up parts from shifting as you clamp them together, first drive several wire brads into the adjoining surfaces. Snip these brads off so they only protrude ¹/₃₂″–¹/₁₆″ above the surface. Dry assemble the parts and press them together until each brad leaves an indentation in the adjoining part. Spread glue on the parts and put them together, sliding them around until you feel the brads find their respective indentations. Then clamp the parts together — the brads will keep them from shifting.

Warning: Don't use this technique if you plan to cut the stock later. You don't want to hit a brad with a saw.

2/Drill a hole in the back of the turkey to mount the tail. Use a doweling jig to make sure this hole is perpendicular to the back surface. If the hole is angled, the tail won't spin properly.

3/Round the parts of the turkey, giving it a realistic shape. Use a rasp to do the rough shaping, then smooth the surface with a file or sandpaper.

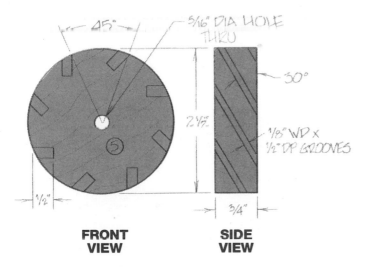

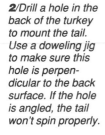

FRONT VIEW   **SIDE VIEW**

HUB LAYOUT

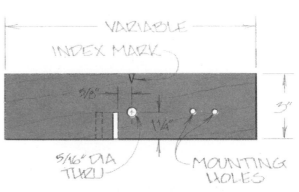

MITER GAUGE EXTENSION LAYOUT

6

Assemble the tail. Press a 5/16″ O.D. roll pin into the hole in the center of the hub. This pin should have an inside diameter slightly larger than 3/16″. It will act as a bushing, helping the tail to turn easily and keeping the wooden hub from wearing away.

Glue the wind vanes into the grooves in the hub. Let the glue dry, then sand the edges of the vanes, blending their contours into the hub.

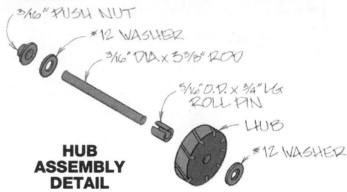

HUB ASSEMBLY DETAIL

7

Assemble the weathercock. Glue the weathercock into its groove in the platform. Reinforce the joint with #8 x 1¼″ flathead wood screws. Counterbore and countersink these screws, then cover the heads with wooden plugs. Sand the plugs flush with the surface of the platform.

Turn the weathercock assembly upside down and drill a ¼″-diameter hole through the edge of the weathercock. Stop the hole at the platform. (See Figure 4.) Using a hacksaw, cut the head off a 10d nail. (This head should be slightly larger than ¼″ in diameter.) Using the shank of the nail, drive the head into the weathercock until it rests at the bottom of the ¼″-diameter hole. This nail head will keep the metal pivot rod from wearing through the wood.

4/To drill the pivot hole in the weathercock, turn the assembly upside down on a drill press. Stop the hole when the drill bit reaches the bottom of the groove in the platform.

8

Assemble the stand (optional). If you want to display this project indoors, you need a stand for it. Bore a ¼″-diameter, 1½″-deep hole in the top end of the post. Taper the post on a band saw, as shown in the *Optional Stand/Side View*. Sand the sawed edges. Glue the bottom of the post to the base, and reinforce it with a #10 x 2″ flathead wood screw.

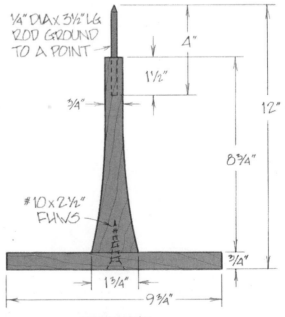

SIDE VIEW OPTIONAL STAND

9

Make the pivot rod. Whether you're displaying the whirligig indoors or out, you'll need a pivot rod. If this will be an inside project, cut the rod 3½" long. If you plan to place it outside, make the rod 7" long. Grind a point on the upper end of the rod with a sander. (See Figure 5.)

*5/To grind a point on the end of the pivot rod, first mount the rod in a hand-held power drill. Hold the free end of the rod at an angle against a belt sander or disk sander so the rotation of the rod **opposes** that of the sander. Let both tools run until a point forms.*

10

Paint the assemblies. Paint the stand (if you've made one), as well as the turkey, tail, and weathercock assemblies. Color the stand to suit your own tastes, and follow the "paint-by-number" code on the *Turkey Pattern, Wind Vane Pattern, Weathercock Pattern,* and *Hub Layout.* Use artist's acrylic paints — they're waterproof and the colors will not fade in the sun or rain.

11

Assemble the turkey, tail, and weathercock. Position the turkey on the platform and lightly mark the position of the feet with a pencil. Drill two ⅛"-diameter holes down through the platform, one for each foot. Center the holes in the foot locations that you've marked.

Glue the turkey assembly to the weathercock assembly. Let the glue dry, then reinforce the glue joints with #10 x 2" flathead wood screws. Countersink the screws, drilling the pilot holes up through the ⅛"-diameter holes that you drilled previously.

Cut the 3/16"-diameter metal tail rod to length and secure one end in the turkey body with epoxy glue. Slide a flat washer over the other end of the rod, then put the tail in place, then add another flat washer. Tap a push nut onto the end of the rod to keep the tail and washers in place.

12

Mount the whirligig. To display this project indoors, place the 3½"-long pivot rod in the top of the stand, pointed end up. Set the whirligig on the stand, inserting the pivot rod in the pivot hole. Check that the whirligig pivots freely.

If you want to display the whirligig outdoors, locate a suitable fence post or wooden structure to mount it, or drive a 2 x 2 treated post in the ground. Bore a ¼"-diameter, 1½"-deep hole in the top of this post or structure. Insert the 7"-long pivot rod in the hole, pointed end up, then set the whirligig on the rod.

TRY THIS! To help the whirligig turn as easily as possible, put a little paste wax in the pivot hole.

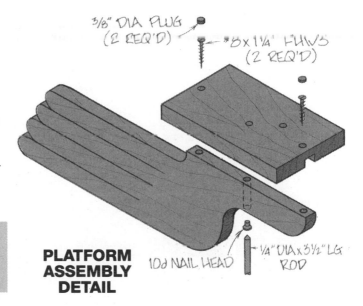

3/8" DIA PLUG (2 REQ'D)

#8 x 1¼" FHWS (2 REQ'D)

10d NAIL HEAD

¼" DIA x 3½" LG ROD

PLATFORM ASSEMBLY DETAIL

Gravity Bookend

Yes, the title of this project is correct: Book-*end,* singular. Traditionally, bookends come in sets of two, of course, but this design sits at a slight angle, so the books lean against a single vertical board. Gravity does the work of the missing bookend.

This gravity bookend makes a handy, compact desktop accessory. It will hold several large reference books, without taking up much more desk space than the books themselves. It takes up less space, in fact, than a pair of conventional bookends.

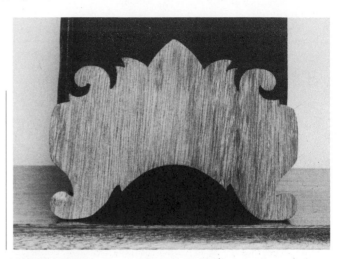

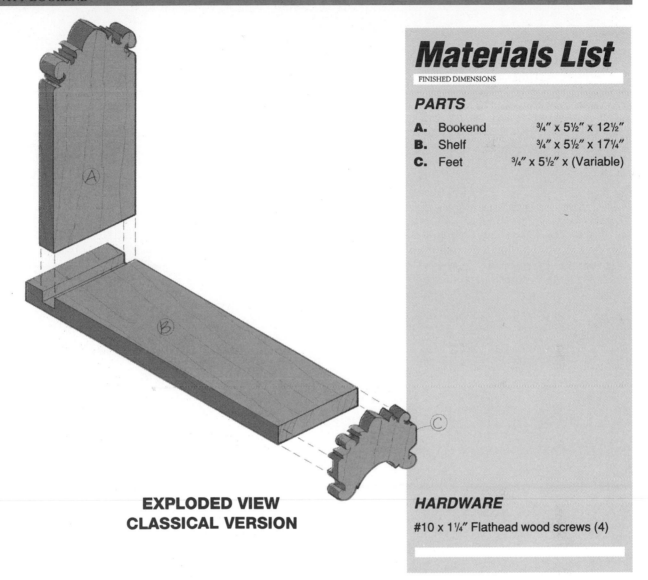

**EXPLODED VIEW
CLASSICAL VERSION**

Materials List

FINISHED DIMENSIONS

PARTS

A.	Bookend	¾" x 5½" x 12½"
B.	Shelf	¾" x 5½" x 17¼"
C.	Feet	¾" x 5½" x (Variable)

HARDWARE

#10 x 1¼" Flathead wood screws (4)

---

1 **Adjust the size and design, as necessary.** As shown, the gravity bookend will hold five 3"-thick books. You can easily adapt it to hold more books simply by lengthening the shelf and raising the feet to keep the shelf angle around 5°. However, don't make it too long. If you stretch the shelf beyond 36", it may sag.

The shapes shown in the photo are classical, drawn from the Chippendale period. Depending on the decor in your office or den, you may prefer a country or contemporary style, as shown in the alternate designs — *Bookend Pattern/Country Version, Feet Pattern/ Country Version, Bookend Pattern/Contemporary Version, and Feet Pattern/Contemporary Version.*

2 **Select the stock and cut it to size.** You can use any cabinet grade hardwood to make this project. Since it's small and requires only three parts, you may want to use scrap wood — this is a good chance to use up some of those shorts you just couldn't

bear to part with. The bookend shown was made of mahogany, left over from a larger project. When you have selected the stock, cut the parts to the sizes in the Materials List. Bevel the bottom edge of the feet to 5°.

3 Cut the dadoes in the shelf and feet.

Using a dado cutter or a router, cut ¾″-wide, ½″- deep dadoes in the shelf and the feet stock, as shown in the *Front View*. The shelf dado holds the bookend, and the feet dado holds the shelf.

Note: Be sure to cut the joinery *before* you cut the patterns. It's difficult to make straight joints once you've cut away the straight edges. It's also possible that you may chip or otherwise damage a delicate shape.

4 Cut the shapes of the bookend and the feet.

Enlarge the *Bookend Pattern* and *Feet Pattern* (any version), and trace these onto the stock.

Cut out the shapes with a band saw or saber saw. Sand the sawed edges smooth.

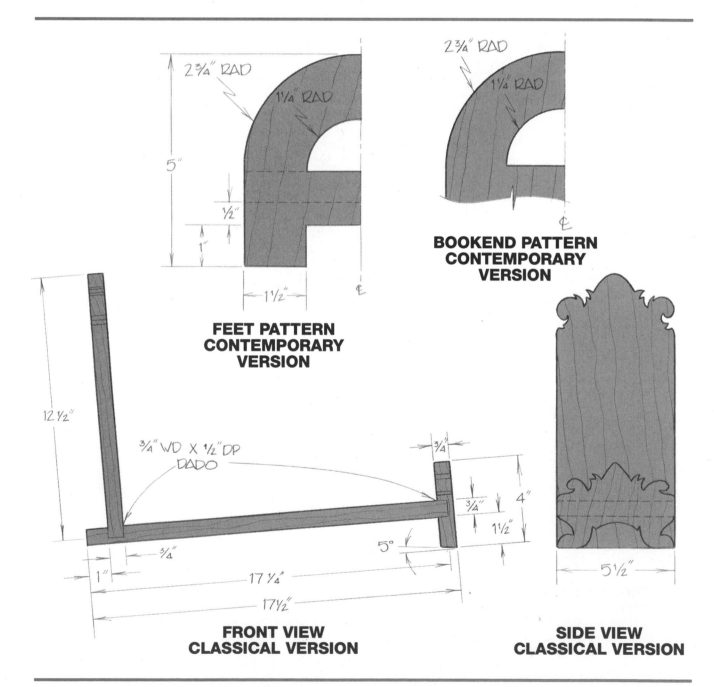

FEET PATTERN CONTEMPORARY VERSION

BOOKEND PATTERN CONTEMPORARY VERSION

FRONT VIEW CLASSICAL VERSION

SIDE VIEW CLASSICAL VERSION

5

Assemble the parts. Finish sand all three parts. Glue the bookend in the shelf dado and the shelf in the feet dado. Wipe away any glue that squeezes out of the joints with a wet rag. Reinforce the joints with flathead wood screws. Counterbore and countersink the screws, then cover the heads with wooden plugs. Sand the plugs flush with the surface.

6

Finish the bookend. Do any necessary touch-up sanding. If you've made the country or the contemporary versions, you may want to round over the edges slightly. Then apply paint, stain, or a clear finish to the completed bookend

TRY THIS! The project shown was finished with hand-rubbed wax. Mix equal parts of turpentine and beeswax and let the concoction sit until it becomes a soft paste. Apply the paste to the wood with a clean cloth and buff it out. Repeat, until the wax builds up to a pleasant shine. Many eighteenth- and nineteenth-century pieces of classical furniture were finished in this manner to bring out the color and grain of the wood.

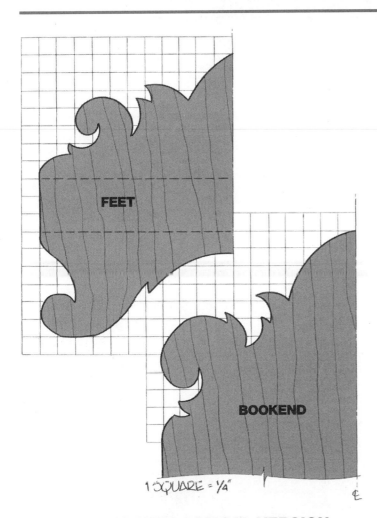

1 SQUARE = ¼"

PATTERN/CLASSICAL VERSION

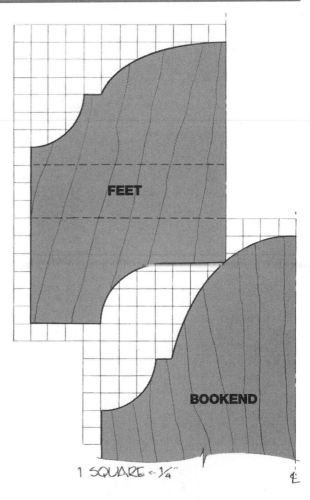

1 SQUARE = ¼"

PATTERN/COUNTRY VERSION

Glazed Wall Cabinet

Glass-front or "glazed" cabinets such as this were prized possessions in early America. Glass was a rare, expensive commodity, since there were only a few foundries in the American colonies.

In addition, these foundries could cast only small panes. The technology of glass casting was not sufficiently advanced to make large ones. Even if it had been, the bigger panes might have broken during the long, jolting wagon ride to market. Consequently, early American cabinetmakers inset several small panes inside a door frame to fill up the space, using a system of delicate rails and stiles to hold the glass. The joinery used to assemble this intricate glazing work was difficult and exacting and sometimes added more to the price of the cabinet than the glass itself.

There were exceptions, however. Country cabinet-makers developed an uncomplicated design for clients who could not afford elaborate glazing work. The door on this small, country-style cabinet is an example. The glazing rails and stiles simply butt together and are glued in the door frame. The rest of the cabinet construction is almost as easy — the larger parts are nailed together — making it possible to build this piece with little more work than a cabinet with a solid door.

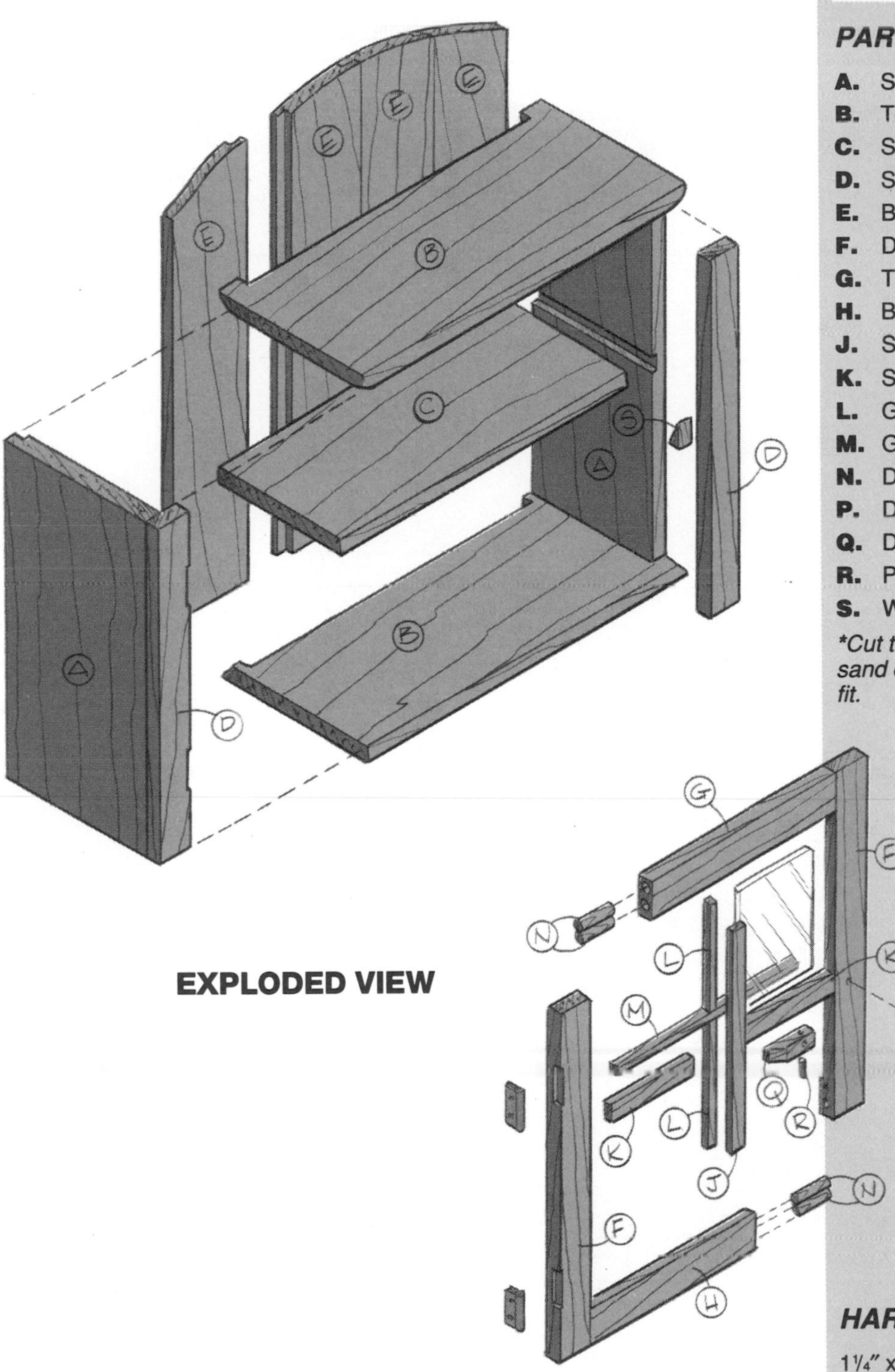

Materials List

FINISHED DIMENSIONS

PARTS

A.	Sides (2)	3/4" x 8" x 19½"
B.	Top/bottom (2)	3/4" x 9½" x 21"
C.	Shelf	3/4" x 7½" x 18½"
D.	Stiles (2)	3/4" x 2" x 19½"
E.	Back boards (4)	½" x 5" x 24"
F.	Door stiles (2)	3/4" x 1¾" x 19½"*
G.	Top door rail	3/4" x 1¾" x 12"*
H.	Bottom door rail	3/4" x 2½" x 12"*
J.	Sash stile	3/8" x 3/4" x 15¼"
K.	Sash rails (2)	3/8" x 3/4" x 55/8"
L.	Glazing stiles (2)	¼" x 3/8" x 153/4"
M.	Glazing rail	¼" x 3/8" x 12½"
N.	Dowels (8)	3/8" dia. x 2"
P.	Door pull	1¼" dia. x 25/8"
Q.	Door latch	½" x 1" x 25/8"
R.	Pin	¼" dia. x 1"
S.	Wedge	¼" x 1" x 1½"

Cut these parts to this length, then sand or plane the assembled door to fit.

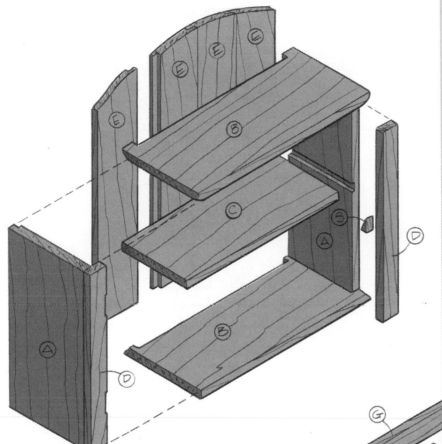

EXPLODED VIEW

HARDWARE

1¼" x 2" Butt hinges and mounting screws (2)
4d Square-cut nails (40–48)
1/8" x 6" x 75/8" Glass panes (4)
Glazing compound

1

Select the stock and cut the parts to size. To build this project, you need about 14 board feet of 4/4 (four-quarters) lumber and a scrap of 8/4 (eight-quarters). You can use any cabinet-grade wood for this project, although old-time country craftsmen normally worked in native American woods such as walnut, cherry, maple, poplar, and white pine. The cabinet shown is made from poplar, then stained dark red and finished with "crackle" lacquer.

When you have selected the wood, cut the parts to the sizes given in the Materials List, except the door pull, wedge, sash rails, sash stile, and other glazing work. Cut a 1½″ x 1½″ x 3½″ block for the door pull — the extra stock will give you room to work when you mount the wood on the lathe. Wait and cut the wedge from a scrap after you've assembled the case and door. Cut the glazing work to the proper thickness and width, but don't cut the parts to length yet.

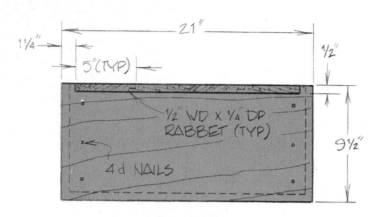

TOP VIEW

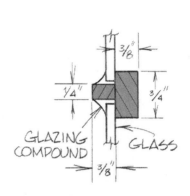

SECTION A

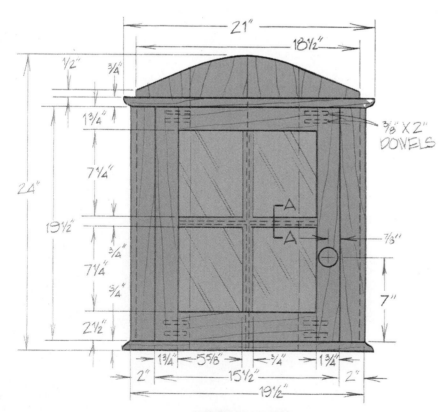

FRONT VIEW

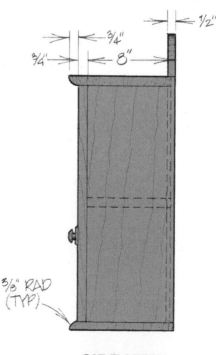

SIDE VIEW

2

Cut the dadoes and rabbets. The parts of the case are assembled with simple dadoes and rabbets. Cut the following joints:

- ¾"-wide, ¼"-deep dadoes in the sides to hold the shelf, as shown in the *Side Layout*
- ½"-wide, ¼"-deep rabbets in the back edges of the sides to hold the back boards

- ½"-wide, ¼"-deep rabbets in the edges of the back boards so they will overlap

Note: Rabbet just *one* edge of the two outside back boards, and *both* edges of the inside back boards, as shown in the *Top View*. The boards will lap each other, forming a solid panel.

3

Shape the edges of the top and bottom. The front edges and both ends of the top and bottom are rounded over, as shown in the *Side View*. Do the rounding with a router and a ⅜" quarter-round bit.

4

Cut the notches in the top and bottom. The back edges of both the top and bottom are notched to fit around the back boards, as shown in the *Top View*. Cut these ½"-wide, 18½"-long notches with a band saw or a saber saw.

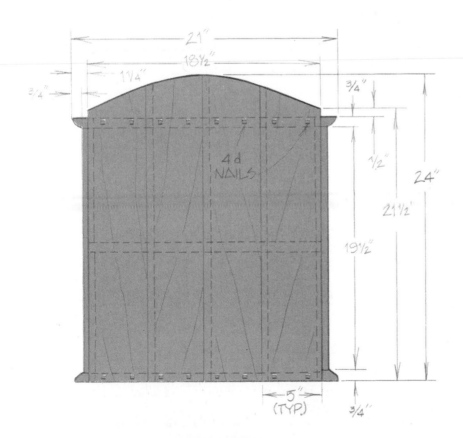

BACK VIEW

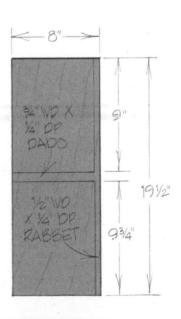

SIDE LAYOUT

5 **Mortise the stiles for hinges.** The inside edge of the left stile and the outside edge of the left door stile must be mortised for hinges. It's easier to cut these mortises now, before you've assembled the case and the door. Carefully measure the locations of the hinges, then trace the outlines of the hinge leaves on the edge of each part. Using a chisel and a routing plane (if you have one), cut mortises that are as deep as the leaves are thick.

6 **Assemble the case.** Finish sand the parts of the case, then assemble them with glue and nails. First, glue the stiles to the front edges of the sides. Let the glue dry and attach the shelf between the sides. Then glue the top and bottom to the sides and stiles. Reinforce all the glue joints with square-cut nails. (See Figure 1.)

Stain the rabbeted edges of the back boards a dark color. This will keep you from seeing light-colored raw wood when the boards contract in cool, dry weather. Nail (but do *not* glue) the back boards to the case. The nails will flex slightly as the boards move with changes in humidity.

1/*To drive a square-cut nail, first drill a pilot hole slightly smaller in diameter than the shaft of the nail (measured halfway along its length). Otherwise, the nail will act as a tiny wedge and split the wood apart. Drive the nail into the pilot hole, then set the head.*

7 **Cut the shape of the back.** The back boards extend above the top to create a backstop, and they are crested slightly for decoration. Enlarge the *Back Pattern* and trace it onto the back surface of the boards. Cut the pattern with a coping saw or saber saw. (See Figure 2.) Sand the sawed edges.

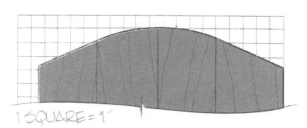

1 SQUARE = 1"

BACK PATTERN

2/*Cut a crest at the top of the back boards **after** you have attached them to the case.*

8 **Assemble the door frame.** The door rails and stiles are assembled with dowel joints. Lay out the door frame parts on your workbench, butting the ends of the rails against the edges of the stiles where you want to attach them. Mark the locations of the dowels. (The precise locations aren't critical, but you should install two dowels in each joint.) Drill ³/₈″-diameter, 1″-deep dowel holes in the parts, using a doweling jig to guide the drill. You can also use mortises and tenons or wooden plates ("biscuits").

Also, drill a ⁹/₁₆″-diameter hole through the right door stile, 7″ from the bottom end. This hole will hold the door pull.

Finish sand the door rails and stiles, and assemble the door frame with glue and dowels. Let the glue dry for at least 24 hours, then sand the joints clean and flush.

9

Rabbet the door frame. The inside edge of the assembled door frame is rabbeted to hold the glass and glazing work. Cut this ¼"-wide, ⅜" deep rabbet with a hand-held router and a *piloted* rabbeting bit. (See Figure 3.) Square the corners of the rabbet with a chisel.

*3/Rout a rabbet in the inside edges of the door frame **after** you've assembled it. Square the round corners of the rabbet with a chisel.*

10

Install the glazing work. Carefully cut the sash stile, sash rails, glazing stiles, and glazing rail to fit inside the frame. The fit should be snug enough that the parts will stay put without glue, but not so tight that the parts bow. (See Figure 4.)

After cutting the parts to the proper length, glue them in the frame. Glue the glazing rail in place first. Let the glue set about a half hour, then glue the sash stile in the frame. Again, let the glue set, then add the glazing stiles and sash rails. Make sure that the glazing work divides the frame into four equal parts. When the glue dries, sand the joints clean and flush.

*4/Cut the glazing work to length **after** you've rabbeted the door frame. These parts should fit snugly enough that they will stay in place without glue.*

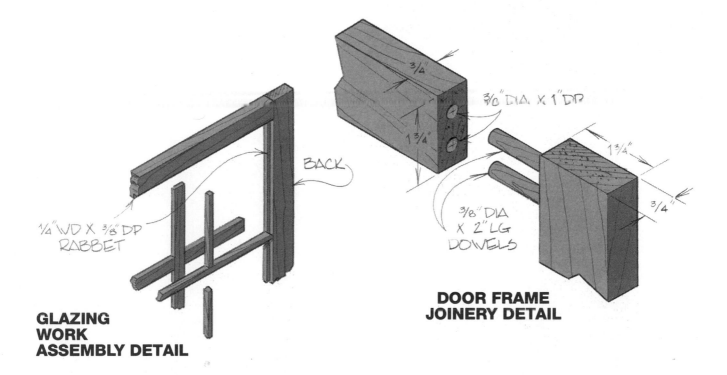

BACK

¼" WD X ⅜" DP RABBET

¾

¾

1¾"

⅜" DIA. X 1" DP

1¾"

¾"

⅜" DIA X 2" LG DOWELS

GLAZING WORK ASSEMBLY DETAIL

DOOR FRAME JOINERY DETAIL

11

Turn the door pull. Turn the door pull on
a lathe to the shape shown in the *Door Pull
Layout*. Finish sand the pull on the lathe.

If you don't have a lathe or don't want to take the
time to turn the pull, you can assemble a pull by drilling
a 1/2″-diameter, 1/2″-deep hole in the back side of a 1 1/4″-
diameter wooden knob. Glue a 1/2″-diameter, 3 1/8″-long
dowel in this hole. When the glue dries, cut the dowel
off so the assembly is 2 5/8″ long.

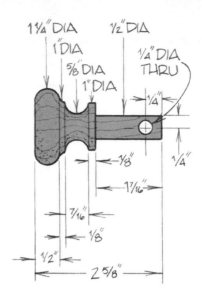

DOOR PULL LAYOUT

12

Mount the door. Sand the top, bottom,
and *right* edges of the door so it fits in the case
with a 1/16″-wide gap all around the perimeter. (Do *not*
sand the left edge; otherwise, you'll have to recut the
hinge mortises.) When the door fits properly, install
hinges and mount it in the case.

Temporarily insert the door pull through the hole in
the right stile. Drill a 1/2″-diameter hole through the
door latch and chamfer one end, as shown in the *Door
Latch Assembly Detail*. Drill a 1/4″-diameter hole
through the latch and pull shaft. Insert (but do *not* glue)
a 1/4″-diameter pin in this hole.

Cut the wedge from a scrap and sand it smooth. Glue
it to the back surface of the right stile, just opposite the
door pull. Clamp it in place while the glue dries by turning the door pull until the latch is snug against the wedge.

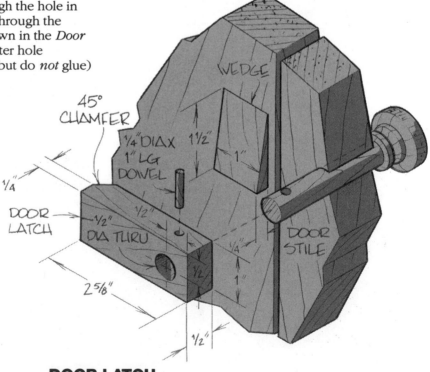

**DOOR LATCH
ASSEMBLY DETAIL**

13 **Finish the cabinet.** Disassemble the door pull, door latch, and pin. Remove the door from the cabinet and the hinges from the door. If you wish, cover the heads of the nails with putty. Do any necessary touch-up sanding, then apply paint or a finish to all the wooden surfaces.

14 **Install the glass in the door.** When the finish dries, replace the door on the case. Assemble the door pull, latch, and pin with glue. Make sure you don't get any glue on the door stile or in the door pull hole — the pull and latch should turn freely.

Mount the glass in the door, keeping it in place with glazing compound. If you wish, mix the compound with stain, aniline dye, or artist's oil paints to match the finish.

Step-by-Step: Cutting Hinge Mortises

One of the most exacting jobs in woodworking is hanging a door from ordinary butt hinges. You must carefully measure the location of the hinges and cut several *hinge mortises* — recesses in the door frame and face frame for the hinge leaves. Not only must these mortises be placed precisely, they must also be cut to a precise depth. In most cases, the depth must match the thickness of the leaves. This is not difficult work, but it's time-consuming and requires patience.

Here are several techniques you can use to speed this process and enhance the precision:

When positioning the hinges, measure their location on the face frame *only*. Fit the door to the cabinet, wedging it in place with toothpicks or slivers of wood. There should be an even 1/16"-wide gap between the face frame and the door frame all around the door. Then *transfer* the position of each hinge to the door frame.

1

Fold a hinge over the edge of the face frame or door frame where you want to install it. Trace around the leaf with a sharp awl or knife, scribing a shallow groove.

2

Rest the edge of a chisel in the groove you made with the awl. Lightly tap the chisel with a mallet, cutting 1/16"–1/8" into the wood and cleanly severing the wood fibers. Do this all around the mortise.

(Continued)

Step-by-Step: Cutting Hinge Mortises — Continued

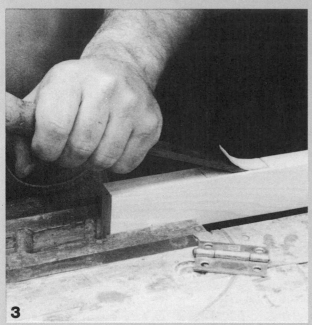

3

Rough out the mortise, removing **most** of the waste with the chisel. If necessary, cut the edges deeper as you remove more stock. Stop when the mortise is within $1/64''$–$1/32''$ of the required depth.

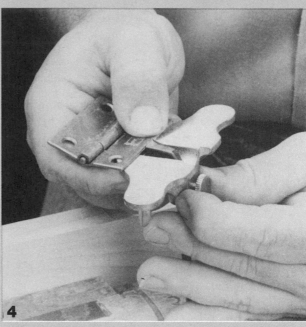

4

Adjust the blade of a router plane to cut as deep as the hinge leaf is thick. You can do this without measuring — just hold the hinge leaf flush against the bottom of the plane and raise or lower the plane iron.

5

Use the plane to remove the last little bit of stock from the bottom of the mortise. The plane will cut a flat-bottomed mortise to an even depth. When you test fit the hinge, the top surface of the leaf should be flush with the wood.

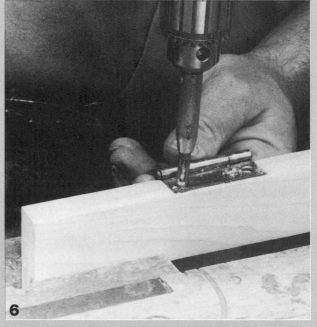

6

Put one hinge leaf in its mortise and, once again, fold the other leaf over the edge of the stock. Using a self-centering bit, drill pilot holes for the screws. Repeat these steps for all the mortises in both the door frame and the face frame, then mount the door. The fit should be perfect — just as it was when you wedged it in place.

Compound-Cut Reindeer

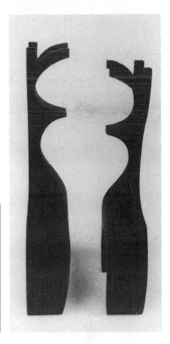

Compound cutting is a simple (but intriguing) band saw technique. Cut a design in one surface of a board, tape the parts back together, then cut a second design in another surface. When you remove the tape and the waste, you'll have a wooden shape that appears to be carved.

This technique is most commonly used to make S-shaped cabriole legs for traditional tables and chairs. However, you can also use compound cuts to create band saw "sculptures" — these reindeer are one example. Each of the animal shapes shown were created by making two sets of band saw cuts in two faces of a single block of wood.

Materials List

FINISHED DIMENSIONS

PARTS

A. Large reindeer   1³/₄″ x 5¹/₄″ x 11″
B. Small reindeer   1⁵/₈″ x 4⁷/₈″ x 9¹/₂″

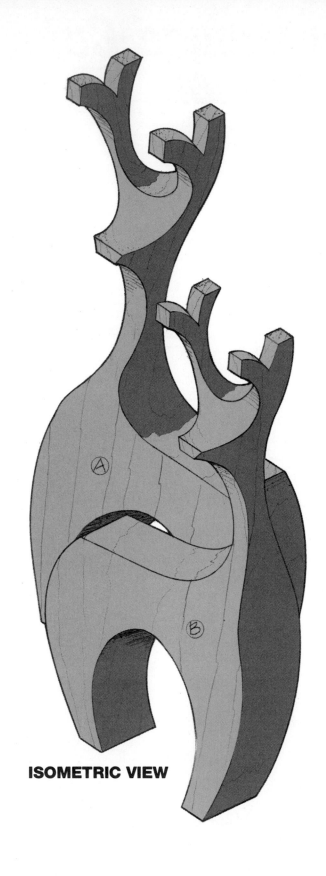

ISOMETRIC VIEW

1

Select and prepare the stock. Each reindeer requires about 1 board foot of 8/4 (eight-quarters) lumber. You can also laminate 4/4 (four-quarters) lumber. These reindeer are made from walnut, but you can use almost any cabinet-grade wood. However, avoid woods that split easily, such as redwood and cedar. Because of the wood grain direction, the antlers are fairly fragile, and a slight bump might break them off a redwood or cedar reindeer.

When you have selected the stock, plane it and cut it to the thickness and length specified in the Materials List. However, rip it ¼"–½" wider than specified. This will give you some extra room when laying out and cutting the shapes.

2

Make two templates for each size of deer. Decide what size of reindeer you want to make — large or small, or both. Enlarge the patterns, trace them on a heavy piece of poster board, and cut them out with a scissors. Or, if you wish to make several copies of the animals, trace the patterns on a piece of hardboard and cut them out with a scroll saw. Sand the sawed edges smooth.

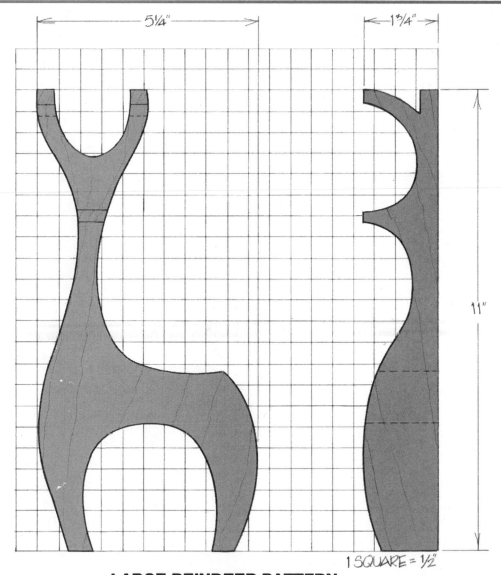

1 SQUARE = ½"

LARGE REINDEER PATTERN

3

Make the first set of cuts. Trace the side pattern or profile onto the edge of the stock. With the stock turned on edge, make the first set of cuts in the order shown in *First Cuts*. (See Figure 1.) Save the scrap from cuts number 3, 4, and 5. Tape these waste pieces back to the stock to make it rectangular again. (See Figure 2.)

TRY THIS! Rather than wrapping the stock in masking tape, use double-faced carpet tape to secure the waste to the stock. This has two advantages. First, the waste won't come loose when you cut through the tape. Second, the tape is about the same thickness as the saw kerf for most small band saw blades; this helps to restore the stock to its original dimensions for the second set of cuts.

1/Make the first set of cuts in the edge of the stock, saving the scrap except for the little piece from between the points of the antlers.

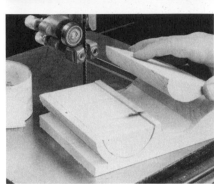

2/Tape the waste you've saved back to the stock, making it rectangular again. Some woodworkers prefer to use double-faced carpet tape for this step.

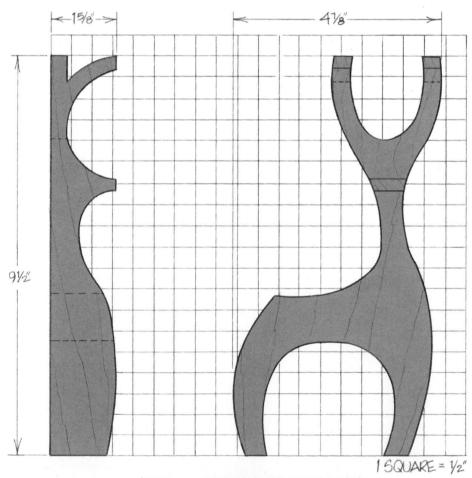

1 SQUARE = ½"

SMALL REINDEER PATTERN

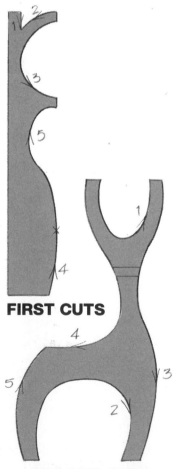

FIRST CUTS

SECOND CUTS

4

Make the second set of cuts. Trace the front pattern on the face of the stock. With the stock resting on the other face, make the second set of cuts in the order shown in *Second Cuts*. (See Figure 3.) Remove the waste and the tape. The remaining stock will be in the rough form of a reindeer. (See Figure 4.)

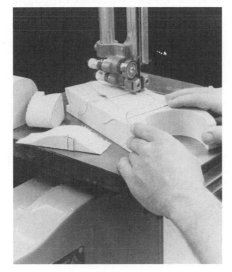

3/Make the second set of cuts in the face of the stock. Don't bother saving the scrap this time.

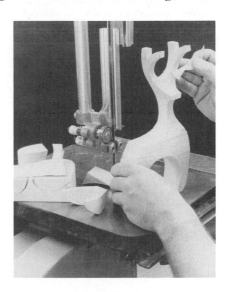

4/Remove any remaining waste and tape to reveal the rough shape of a reindeer.

5

Sand and finish the reindeer. Carefully sand the surfaces of the reindeer to remove the saw marks. (See Figure 5.) Be particularly careful when sanding the antlers. As mentioned previously, these may break off easily.

After sanding the reindeer smooth, apply a finish. The finish shown is a hand-rubbed oil, but you may use any suitable finish, stain, or paint.

TRY THIS! On the reindeer shown, the corners were left fairly "hard" to give them a contemporary look. You may wish to soften the corners or round them over completely. Make several test deer from white pine or another easily shaped wood and experiment until you get the look you want.

5/Carefully sand the surfaces of the reindeer smooth. A set of small drum sanders will help speed this step.

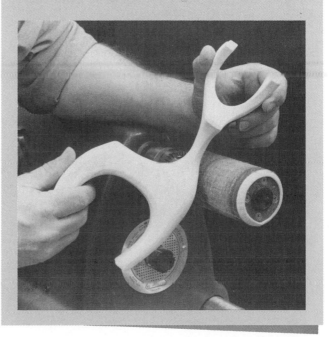

Doll Cradle

Every doll needs a cradle — just ask any child. How else do you rock your playmate to sleep? This half-size cradle, patterned after a traditional Early American design, provides a comfortable place for a doll to bed down.

This miniature cradle can also be used as a holder for flower arrangements or to display stuffed animals. Or, it can serve as a catchall for magazines, toys, knitting, and other small items. Doll or no doll, a doll cradle has many imaginative uses.

Although it may look difficult to build, this particular cradle is easier to make than most. It's just an open box on rockers, assembled with some imaginative joinery. The corners, which seem to be joined with traditional dovetails, are actually *keyed* together. With the help of a simple router jig, you can make and install these dovetail-shaped keys in minutes.

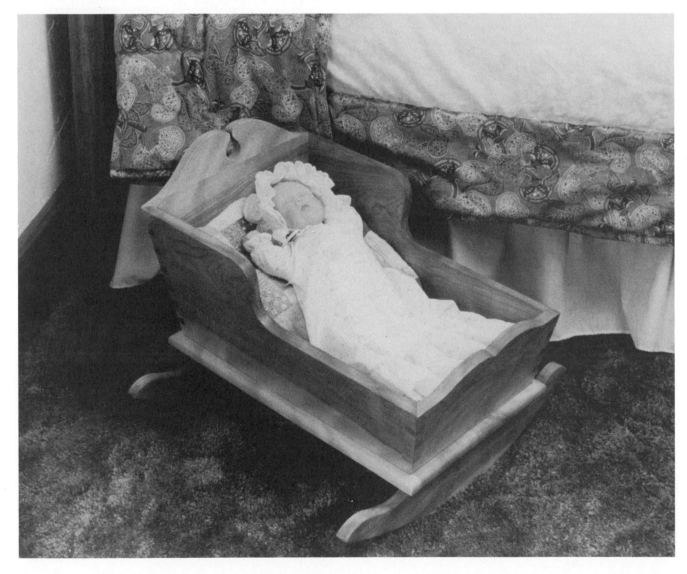

Materials List

FINISHED DIMENSIONS

PARTS

A. Headboard $5/8'' \times 10\,1/2'' \times 12\,3/8''$

B. Footboard $5/8'' \times 5\,3/8'' \times 11\,1/4''$

C. Sides (2) $5/8'' \times 8'' \times 18\,3/8''$

D. Bottom $5/8'' \times 11'' \times 17\,1/2''$

E. Rockers (2) $5/8'' \times 4'' \times 18''$

F. Brace $5/8'' \times 2'' \times 14\,1/2''$

G. Dovetail keys (18) $7/16'' \times 1/2'' \times 1''*$

*Cut the splines to this length initially, then sand them to their proper length **after** you install them.*

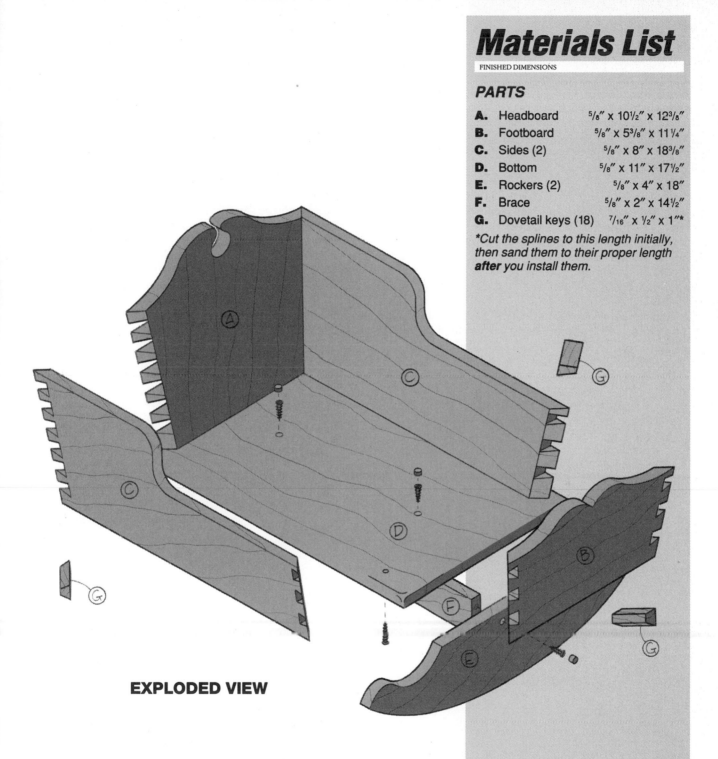

EXPLODED VIEW

HARDWARE

#8 x 1¼″ Flathead wood screws (6)
#8 x 1¼″ Roundhead wood screws (8)
#8 Flat washers (8)

1 **Select the stock and cut it to size.** To make this project, you'll need approximately 8 board feet of 4/4 (four-quarters) lumber. The cradle shown is made from curly birch; however, you can use any cabinet-grade wood. If you plan to paint the cradle, use an inexpensive wood such as poplar or pine.

Plane the lumber to ⅝" thick. Cut the bottom and the brace to the sizes shown in the Materials List. Cut the headboard, footboard, sides, and rockers ½" to 1" longer and wider than specified to give yourself room to saw the shapes. Don't cut the dovetail keys at this time — you'll make these from scraps later on.

2 **Miter and bevel the headboard, footboard, and sides.** The headboard, footboard, and sides are joined to each other with *compound* miters — the ends of the boards are mitered *and* beveled. They are also beveled where they join the bottom. Make all of these cuts on a table saw or radial arm saw.

Make the compound miters first. Tilt the blade of the table saw to 44¼°, and the miter gauge to 80¼°. (If you're using a radial arm saw, tilt the blade to 44¼° and angle the arm at 80¼°.) *Don't cut the good stock* until you've first tested the blade and miter gauge settings on scrap stock. These angles are right out of a textbook and only apply if your saw and saw blade are *perfectly* aligned and adjusted. You may have to readjust the settings slightly to compensate for the idiosyncrasies of your machine.

Compound-miter four pieces of scrap stock so they are all *exactly* the same length. Dry assemble these scrap parts with tape. (See Figure 1.) Check the corner joints and the slope of the sides. If the joints gap on the *outside, increase* the blade tilt. If they gap on the *inside, reduce* the blade tilt. If the slope is less than 10° (off vertical), *reduce* the miter gauge angle. If the slope is *more, increase* the miter gauge angle. Make very small adjustments, no more than ¼° at a time.

Compound-miter the same scrap again with the new settings, shaving about ¼" off the length. Dry assemble the scraps again, and readjust the setting, if necessary. Continue until you get a perfect fit. *Then* compound-miter the headboard, footboard, and sides. (See Figure 2.)

Dry assemble the headboard, footboard, and sides with tape in the same manner that you assembled the scraps. Mark the inside and outside surfaces of each part. Disassemble the parts and bevel-cut the *bottom* edges at 10°.

1/Before compound-mitering the good stock, test the blade tilt and miter gauge angle by cutting four scraps. Dry assemble the scraps with tape to check the fit of the miter joints.

2/When you're sure that the blade and the miter gauge are set properly, compound-miter the headboard, footboard, and sides.

3 **Cut the shapes of the headboard, footboard, sides, and rockers.** Enlarge the *Headboard Pattern, Footboard Pattern, Side Pattern,* and *Rocker Pattern.* Trace these onto the stock, then dry assemble the headboard, footboard, and side parts again to check that all the top edges will be flush after you cut the shapes.

Cut the shapes with a band saw, saber saw, or scroll saw. Sand the sawed edges to remove the saw marks.

TRY THIS!   To save time, "pad saw" and "pad sand" the sides and rockers. Stack the parts face to face and tape them together so they won't shift. Cut the shapes of both sides and both rockers at once. Leave the parts taped together while you sand the edges.

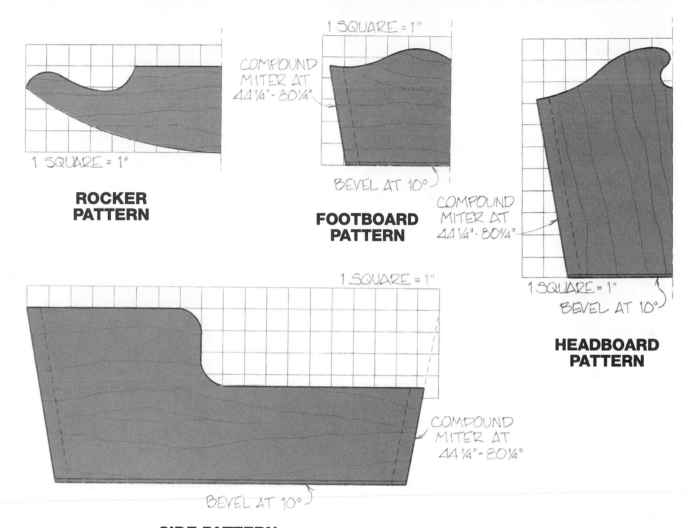

ROCKER PATTERN

1 SQUARE = 1"

1 SQUARE = 1"

COMPOUND MITER AT 44¼° - 80¼°

BEVEL AT 10°

FOOTBOARD PATTERN

COMPOUND MITER AT 44¼° - 80¼°

1 SQUARE = 1"

BEVEL AT 10°

HEADBOARD PATTERN

1 SQUARE = 1"

COMPOUND MITER AT 44¼° - 80¼°

BEVEL AT 10°

SIDE PATTERN

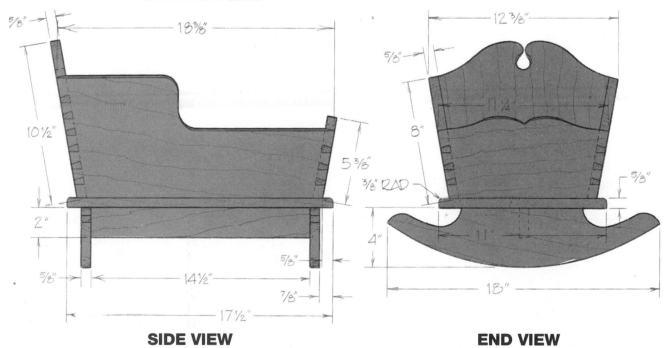

5/8"

18⅜"

10½"

5⅜"

2"

5/8"

14½"

5/8"

7/8"

17½"

SIDE VIEW

12⅜"

5/8"

11¼

8"

3/8" RAD

5/8"

4"

11"

18"

END VIEW

4

Assemble the headboard, footboard, sides, rockers, and brace. Finish sand all the parts you have made so far *except* the bottom. Apply a generous amount of glue to the compound-mitered ends of the headboard, footboard, and sides,

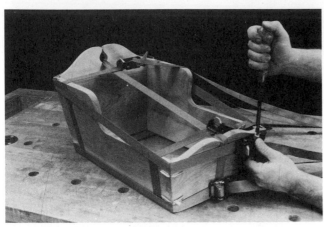

3/To hold the headboard, footboard, and sides together, wrap band clamps around the assembly. The clamps must cross each other, like the ribbons on a gift-wrapped package. If you don't have band clamps, you can use strips of an old inner tube.

then assemble them with tape. Wrap band clamps around the assembly to hold it together while the glue dries. (See Figure 3.) Wipe away any glue that squeezes out of the joints with a wet rag.

After the glue dries, "blend" the top edges of the parts together at the corners. File and sand the edges until they're flush and seem to flow into one another.

Apply glue to the ends of the brace, then clamp the rockers to it. Reinforce the glue joints with wood screws, as shown in the *Rocker Joinery Detail*. Counterbore and countersink the heads of the screws, then cover them with wooden plugs. Again, wipe away any glue that squeezes out of the joints.

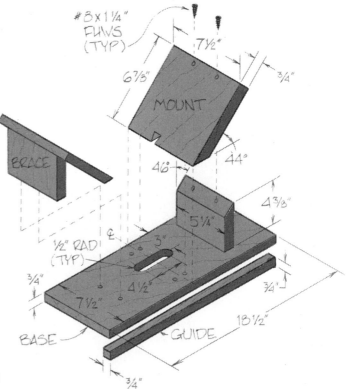

ROCKER JOINERY DETAIL

5

Cut dovetail slots in the corners of the cradle assembly. To install the dovetail keys, you must rout dovetail slots diagonally through the corners of the cradle assembly. And to do this, first make a routing jig, as shown in the *Dovetail Key Jig*. Assemble this jig from scraps of plywood. Note that the mounts are attached to the base at 44°. (The angle between the two mounts is 92°.) These odd angles compensate for the slope on the cradle assembly.

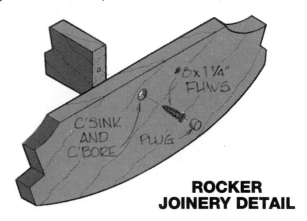

DOVETAIL KEY JIG EXPLODED VIEW

After you've made the jig, clamp the cradle assembly to your workbench and place the jig over one corner. Position it to cut the first slot, and clamp it to the side. Mount a dovetail bit in the router and adjust the depth of cut to make a slot 7/16″ deep. Slide the router across the jig, cutting a slot through the compound-mitered corner. (See Figure 4.) Reposition the jig for the next slot and repeat. Continue until you have cut all the slots in all the corners.

Note: Rout six slots in the corners where the headboard joins the sides, and three slots where the footboard joins the sides. The spacing of these slots is not critical, but they should be fairly even. On the cradle shown, they are about 1″ apart.

4/Cut dovetail slots diagonally across the corners with the aid of a jig. Keep the base of the router pressed firmly against the guide on the base of the jig as you cut.

6 Install the dovetail keys in the slots.

Make the dovetail keys from scrap wood, using the same router bit you used to rout the slots. Keep the bit mounted in the router, then mount the router to a router table. Adjust the height of the dovetail bit so it's 7/16″ above the table. Attach a fence to the table a short distance away from the bit.

Using this fence as a guide, cut one side of the key stock, then turn it over and cut the other. The two cuts will create a dovetail-shaped tenon along one edge of the board. (See Figure 5.) Test fit the tenon in one of the dovetail slots. If it's too *large,* move the fence *closer* to the bit. If it's too *small,* move the fence *farther away.*

When the position of the fence is adjusted properly, rout enough scrap stock to make the keys you'll need.

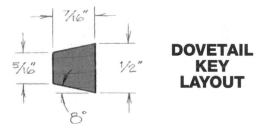

DOVETAIL KEY LAYOUT

Rip the tenons free from the scrap with a band saw or table saw, then cut them up into 1″-long keys.

Glue the keys in the slots. (See Figure 6.) When the glue dries, cut and sand the keys flush with the surface of the cradle assembly.

5/To make the keys, use the dovetail router bit to cut a dovetail-shaped tenon along the edge of a scrap board. Feed the board so the rotation of the bit helps to hold it against the fence. After you've made the tenon, rip it from the board and cut it into 1″-long dovetail-shaped keys.

6/Glue the keys in the slots. After the glue dries, cut the protruding parts of the keys off with a dovetail saw and sand them flush with the surface of the cradle assembly.

7

Round the edges and ends of the bottom. Using a router and a ³⁄₈″ quarter-round bit, round over the edges of the bottom as shown in the *End View* and *Side View*. Sand the edges smooth, and finish sand the bottom.

8

Attach the assemblies to the bottom. Attaching the cradle and rocker assemblies to the bottom presents a problem: If you glue the assemblies to the bottom, or attach them tightly with screws, the bottom will not be able to expand and contract with changes in humidity. The grain direction of the headboard, footboard, and rockers is perpendicular to the grain of the bottom, and this will restrict the movement of the bottom. Eventually, the project will warp or distort and the bottom may split.

To prevent this, attach the assemblies to the bottom with screws in *slots* instead of holes. You can secure the assemblies to the *middle* of the bottom with flathead screws in ordinary counterbored, countersunk pilot holes. However, use roundhead screws and washers to attach the assemblies near the edges of the bottom, as shown in the *Bottom Layout/Bottom View*. The bottom will be able to expand and contract from the middle.

To make the slotted counterbores, first drill ⁵⁄₈″-diameter, ¹⁄₄″-deep holes. Inside each of these stopped holes, drill two or three ¹⁄₈″-diameter holes in a straight line, perpendicular to the grain direction, so they form a ¹⁄₈″-wide, ¹⁄₄″-long slot as shown in the *Counterbore and Slot Detail*.

Note: You must drill some of the slotted counterbores from the *top surface* of the bottom, and others from the *bottom surface,* as shown in the *Bottom Layout/Bottom View*. All the pilot holes that are both counterbored and countersunk should be drilled from the *top surface*.

Attach the rocker assembly to the bottom first. Drive #8 x 1¼″ flathead wood screws into the brace and into the middle of the rockers. Cover the heads of the screws that hold the brace with plugs, and sand the plugs flush with the surface. Drive roundhead wood screws with washers down through the counterbored slots and into the rockers to the right and left of the middle.

COUNTERSINK

COUNTERBORE
AND
SLOT

COUNTERBORE
AND
COUNTERSINK

BOTTOM LAYOUT
BOTTOM VIEW

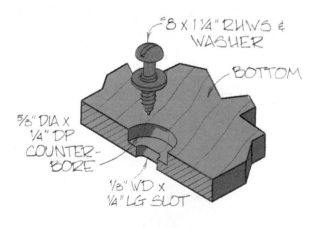

#8 x 1¼″ RHWS & WASHER

BOTTOM

⁵⁄₈″ DIA X
¼″ DP
COUNTER-
BORE

¹⁄₈″ WD X
¼″ LG SLOT

COUNTERBORE
AND SLOT
DETAIL

Clamp the cradle assembly on the bottom. The head-board and footboard should cover the heads of the screws that secure the rocker assembly. Drive round-head wood screws with washers up through the counterbored slots and into the sides, as shown in the *Bottom Joinery Detail*.

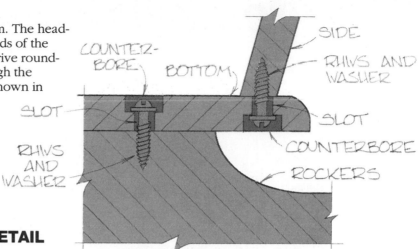

BOTTOM JOINERY DETAIL

9 **Finish the cradle.** Do any necessary touch-up sanding, then apply a finish to the completed cradle. Be careful to coat all surfaces evenly — inside, outside, top, and bottom.

Variations

By adjusting the dimensions of the parts and the number of dovetail keys, you can use this same plan to build a full-size cradle for an infant. Increase the thickness of the stock to ¾″. Lengthen the sides to 40″ and the brace to 35½″. Multiply the other overall dimensions by 1½. Use 12 keys to reinforce each headboard corner, and 6 keys for each footboard corner.

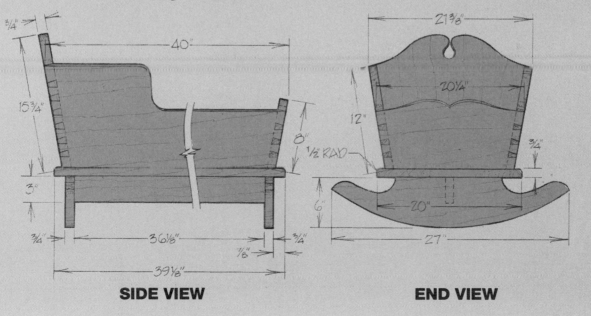

SIDE VIEW   **END VIEW**

Floor-to-Ceiling Bookshelves

If you have a large library, consider covering a whole wall — floor to ceiling — with shelves. This offers two advantages. First, you can get more shelves in a given space. Second, the walls, floor, and ceiling will brace the structure, so you don't need elaborate joinery or bracework; consequently, the case requires less time and fewer materials to build.

The bookcase shown is just a huge box set against a wall. The sides of the box touch opposing walls; the bottom and top touch the floor and ceiling. This keeps the box rigid. The shelves rest on standards and clips, inlaid into the vertical supports of the box. The clips can be easily moved to adjust the shelves. A few screws, driven through the case and into the walls, keep the whole assembly in place. Even though the bookcase has a built-in look, you can easily remove it by loosening these screws.

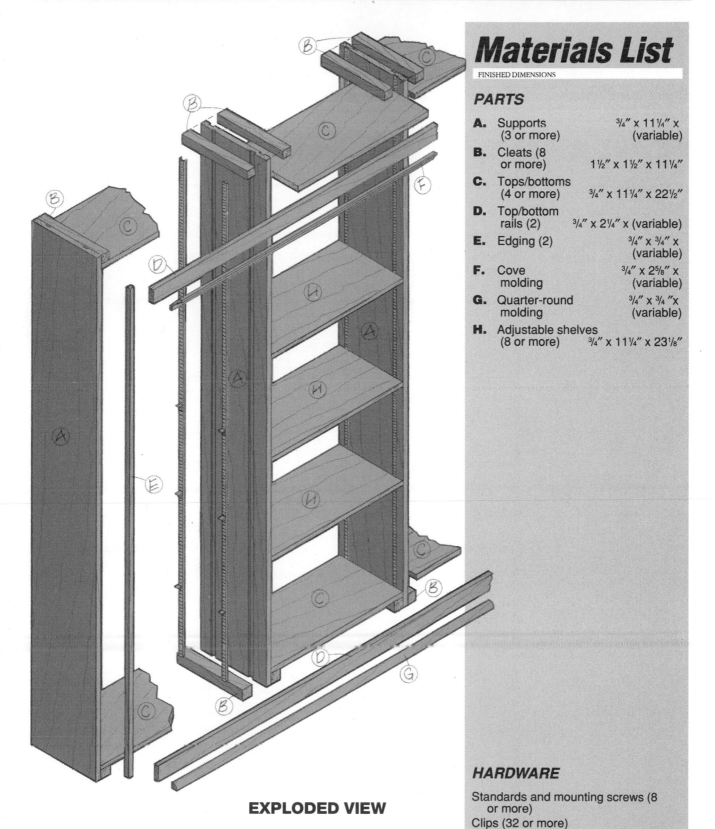

EXPLODED VIEW

Materials List

FINISHED DIMENSIONS

PARTS

A. Supports (3 or more) — ¾″ x 11¼″ x (variable)

B. Cleats (8 or more) — 1½″ x 1½″ x 11¼″

C. Tops/bottoms (4 or more) — ¾″ x 11¼″ x 22½″

D. Top/bottom rails (2) — ¾″ x 2¼″ x (variable)

E. Edging (2) — ¾″ x ¾″ x (variable)

F. Cove molding — ¾″ x 2⅝″ x (variable)

G. Quarter-round molding — ¾″ x ¾″ x (variable)

H. Adjustable shelves (8 or more) — ¾″ x 11¼″ x 23⅛″

HARDWARE

Standards and mounting screws (8 or more)
Clips (32 or more)
6d Finishing nails (1 lb.)
#12 x 2″ Flathead wood screws (8)

1 Determine the size of the bookcase.

Carefully measure the wall where you want to install the bookcase. To determine the size of the bookcase, subtract ⅛″ from the width and height of the space you want to fill.

Make a rough sketch of the bookcase, and write in the measurements. This doesn't have to be anything fancy, just a simple plan to use as a guide when purchasing the wood, cutting the parts, and installing the bookcase.

Note: If the width of the bookcase is not easily divisible by 24″, you will have to decrease the width of one or more sections. You can either make one short section, or make all the sections slightly shorter than 24″. Don't make any shelves longer than 24″, because they may bow.

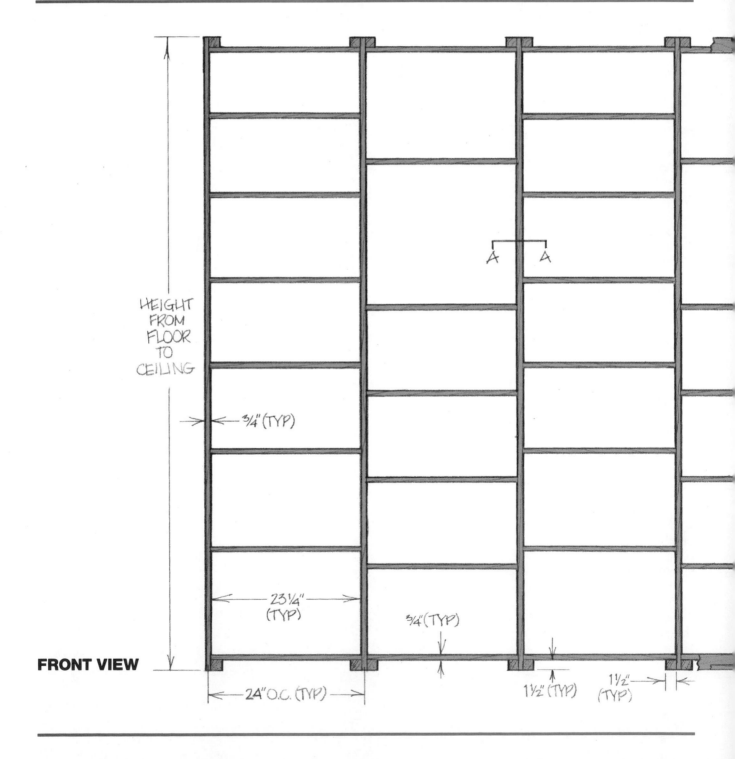

HEIGHT FROM FLOOR TO CEILING

¾″ (TYP)

23¼″ (TYP)

¾″ (TYP)

1½″ (TYP)

1½″ (TYP)

FRONT VIEW

24″ O.C. (TYP)

2 Select the stock and cut the parts to size.

Determine the variables in the Materials List, then figure how much wood you need to build the bookcase. If you're building a large case, you can save money by using cabinet-grade ¾″ plywood instead of hardwood. However, this will require some extra time: You'll have to cover the front edge of every piece with a wooden strip to hide the plies.

Give some careful thought to what color of wood or plywood you want to use. A large, dark bookcase made from mahogany or walnut can be very imposing. It may be okay for a large space, but overwhelming in a smaller room. If the room is small, use a light-colored wood such as birch or pine. The case won't look quite so massive. In an extremely small room, make the bookcase from an inexpensive wood and paint it the same

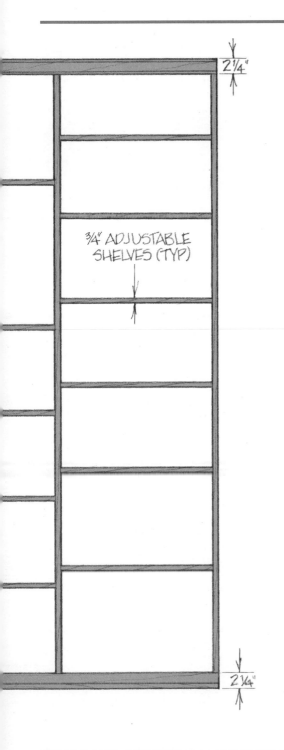

2¼″

¾″ ADJUSTABLE SHELVES (TYP)

2¼″

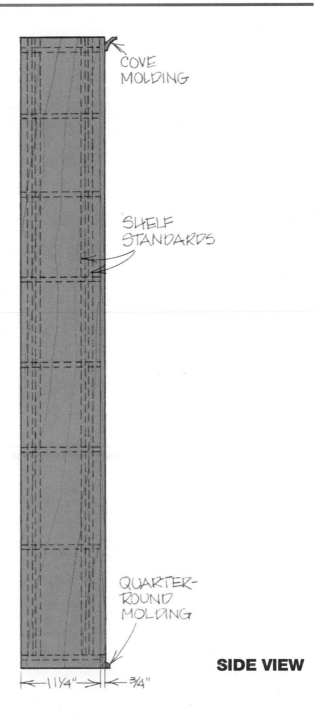

COVE MOLDING

SHELF STANDARDS

QUARTER-ROUND MOLDING

1¼″   ¾″

SIDE VIEW

color as the walls. The case won't seem to take up any space at all.

When you've purchased the wood, cut all the parts to size except the rails, edging, and molding. It's best to

cut these parts *after* you've installed most of the bookcase. When making large, built-in projects such as these, sometimes the measurements change slightly as you assemble them.

3 Cut standard grooves in the supports.

You must set the standards in long grooves so they will be flush with the surface of the supports. Note that the standards should be staggered, as shown in *Section A.* Otherwise, the grooves on either side of a support will leave too little wood remaining, weakening the piece.

Carefully measure the thickness and the width of the metal standards you'll be using. The standards used to make this case were 9⁄16″ wide and 3⁄16″ thick, but yours

may be slightly different. Using a dado cutter or a router and a straight bit, cut grooves in the supports to hold the standards. (See Figure 1.) Cut two grooves in both the right and left sides of the middle supports, as shown in *Section A*. However, cut the inside face only of each end support.

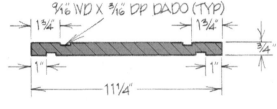

SECTION A

1/Stagger the standard grooves in the middle supports. Don't cut them directly opposite one another — this may weaken the supports.

4 Finish the bookcase and install the standards.

After cutting the grooves, finish sand the supports, the top and bottom sections, and the shelves. Apply a stain, paint, or finish to the parts. You'll

find it's much easier to finish these parts now, rather than wait until you've assembled the bookcase. After the finish dries, install the standards in the grooves with small flathead screws.

5 Attach the cleats to the supports.

Attach the cleats to the ends of the supports with finishing nails. Each middle support requires four cleats — two on either side — and each end support requires two cleats. The cleats must be flush with the ends of the supports.

Note: *Don't* glue the cleats in place. The finishing nails give slightly as the supports expand and contract with changes in temperature and humidity. If you glue the cleats to them, the supports won't be able to "breathe." Eventually, they may warp or split.

6 Prepare the space where you will install the bookcase.

Remove the wall moldings from the space where you want to build the

bookcase so it will fit flat against the walls. Paint the walls and ceiling if needed; the room will be much harder to paint when the bookcase is installed.

7 **Install the supports.** Put the end supports in place. Press them against the walls, then drive several screws through each support and into a stud in the wall. With a helper, position one of the middle sup-

ports. Using finishing nails, attach a top and a bottom to the cleats, tying an end support to the middle support. Repeat until you have installed all the middle supports, tops, and bottoms.

---

8 **Make the rails, edging, and moldings.** Measure the bookcase — chances are the dimensions will have changed slightly from what you originally planned. Then cut the stock for the rails, edging, and cove molding. Cut a board to length for the quarter-round molding, but don't rip it to the proper width yet.

To make the quarter-round molding, round over the edge of the stock with a shaper or router. Then rip the molding to the proper width. (See Figure 2.)

To make the cove molding, you must first cut a cove with a table saw. Place a straightedge on the table of the saw, 23° off parallel to the blade and adjusted to guide the stock over the center of the blade. Clamp the straightedge to the table. Lower the saw blade until it's cutting no more than ⅛" deep. Feed the molding stock across the saw blade, guiding it along the straightedge. Raise the blade about ⅛", and make another pass. Continue until the cove is ½" deep. (See Figure 3.)

Once you've cut the cove, tilt the fence of a jointer toward the knives at a 45° angle. Adjust the depth of cut to ⁵⁄₃₂". Bevel all four corners of the stock, making *two* passes over the knives to cut the *front* corners, and *four* passes to cut the *back* corners. (See Figure 4.) Scrape and sand the concave surface of the molding to remove the saw marks.

*2/When making narrow moldings, always shape the edge of a wide board, **then** rip the molding to the proper width. If you attempt to shape a narrow board, it may snap or splinter as you're working with it.*

3/To make a cove molding, first cut a cove in the front face of the molding stock. Pass the wood over a 10"-diameter table saw, guiding it along a fence set at 23° to the blade. Make the cut in several passes, cutting just ⅛" deeper with each pass. Feed the stock very slowly across the blade.

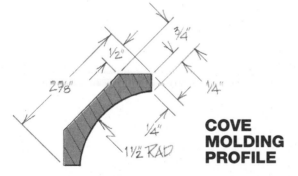

COVE MOLDING PROFILE

2⅞" · ½" · ¾" · ¼" · ¼" · 1½ RAD

4/Finish the cove molding by beveling all four corners at 45° on a jointer. Cut a wider bevel in the back corners than in the front corners.

---

9 **Install the rails, edging, moldings, and shelves.** Finish sand the rails, edgings, and moldings. Apply a finish to these parts, matching the shelves and supports. Nail the rails to the cleats, then nail the edgings to the end supports. Finally, nail the moldings to the rails. Set all finishing nails slightly below the surface of the wood. If necessary, touch up

the finish where you may have scratched the wood or hit it with a hammer.

Insert clips in the standards where you want to put shelves. Each shelf must be supported by four clips. Rest the shelves on the clips, then begin putting the room back in order.

Collapsible Candleholder

Most folks have an *occasional* need for candles and candleholders, during formal dinners, special occasions, and power failures. At other times, the candles and candleholders become a storage problem — they simply take up space.

This candleholder takes up less space than most when it's not in use. It folds flat, collapsing to the size of a paperback book. But when it's needed, it expands to hold up to five full-size candles. Furthermore, it can be arranged in several different configurations to complement the decor or fit the available space. You can also combine two or more of these holders for more decorative possibilities — and more candles. ●

Materials List

FINISHED DIMENSIONS

PARTS

A.	Long holder	³/₄″ x 1¹/₂″ x 7¹/₂″
B.	Tall leg	³/₄″ x 1¹/₂″ x 3³/₄″
C.	Medium-long holder	³/₄″ x 1¹/₂″ x 6⁹/₁₆″
D.	Medium-tall leg	³/₄″ x 1¹/₂″ x 3″
E.	Medium holder	³/₄″ x 1¹/₂″ x 5¹¹/₁₆″
F.	Medium leg	³/₄″ x 1¹/₂″ x 2¹/₄″
G.	Medium small holder	³/₄″ x 1¹/₂″ x 4¹³/₁₆″
H.	Medium small leg	³/₄″ x 1¹/₂″ x 1¹/₂″
J.	Small holder	³/₄″ x 1¹/₂″ x 3¹⁵/₁₆″
K.	Small leg	³/₄″ x 1¹/₂″ x ³/₄″
L.	Dowel	¹/₄″ dia. x 4″
M.	Keeper	1¹/₂″ dia. x ³/₄″

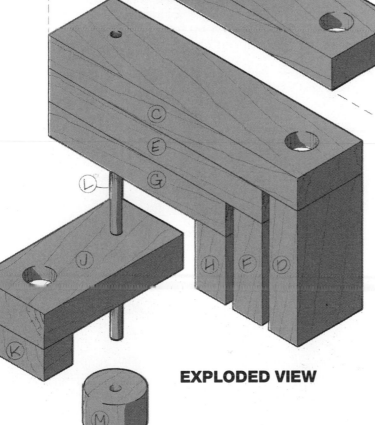

EXPLODED VIEW

1 **Select the stock and cut it to size.** To make this candleholder, you need less than a single board foot of 4/4 (four-quarters) lumber. Because it requires so little material — and because the parts are so small — you may be able to use wood scraps that you've been hoarding. The candleholders shown are made from cherry and walnut, but you can use any cabinet-grade wood.

When you've selected the stock, cut all the parts to the sizes shown in the Materials List.

2 **Cut the keeper.** Mark the round shape of the keeper with a compass, then saw it with a band saw or scroll saw. You may also use a 1³/₄"-diameter hole saw — the waste will be about 1¹/₂" in diameter. Sand the sawed edges of the keeper.

3 **Drill the holes in the holders and the keeper.** Each holder requires two holes — one for the pivot dowel, and another to hold the candle. Make the candle hole first. Drill a ³/₄"-diameter, ⁵/₈"-deep hole in each holder, ³/₄" from one end.

Stack the holders, bottom face up, on top of each other. The longest holder should be on the bottom of the stack, and the shortest on the top. Make sure the edges and the *pivoting* ends (opposite the candle holes) are flush. Then tape the stack together so the parts won't shift. Drill a ¹/₄"-diameter hole, ³/₄" from the pivoting ends, through the bottom, bottom-middle, middle, and top-middle holders. (See Figure 1.) Continue drilling into the top holder, but stop before the drill exits the stock. The hole in the top holder should be just ³/₈" deep, as shown in the *Side View*.

Also, drill a ¹/₄"-diameter, ³/₈"-deep hole in the center of the keeper.

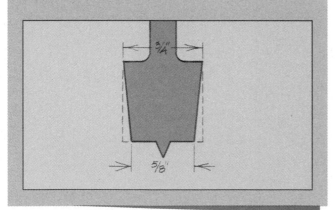

TRY THIS! The ends of most candles are tapered slightly. You can make your own tapered candleholder bit by grinding the sides of a spade bit as shown.

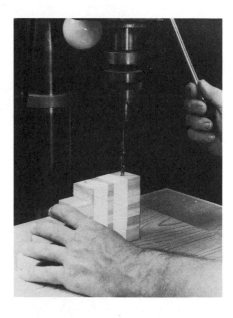

1/To save time, drill the pivot holes in all the holders at the same time.

4 **Assemble the holders and legs.** Finish sand all the parts. Glue the legs to the *candle* ends of the holders. The outside face of each leg must be flush with the end of the holder. Sand the joints clean and flush.

Note: Because these parts are glued end-grain to long-grain, the glue joints are not particularly strong. If you wish, you may reinforce these joints with 4d finishing nails. But unless the candleholder will see hard use, the glue should be enough to hold the parts together.

5 **_Assemble the holders._** Insert the dowel through the pivot holes in the bottom, bottom-middle, middle, and top-middle holders. Glue the top end of the dowel in the stopped pivot hole in the top holder, and the bottom end in the hole in the keeper. Take care not to get any glue on the other holders.

6 **_Finish the candleholder._** Do any necessary touch-up sanding on the completed candleholder. Then apply a finish that _penetrates_ the surface of the wood, such as tung oil or Danish oil. Finishes that build up on the surface, such as varnish or polyurethane, will cause the holders to stick together.

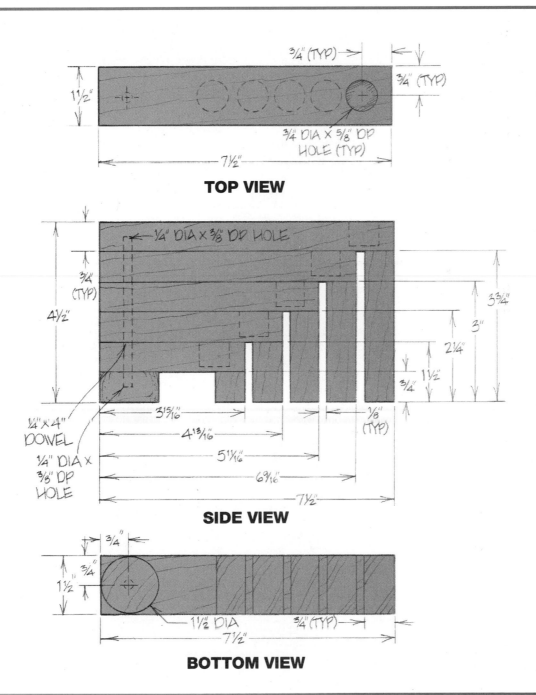

TOP VIEW

SIDE VIEW

BOTTOM VIEW

Turned Boxes

One of the quickest ways to make small boxes is to *turn* them. It's also one of the most creative methods. Fit a lid to a box, then turn the box (with its lid in place) to almost any shape you want. This doesn't require any special equipment, other than a lathe and a lathe chuck.

The boxes shown are the creation of Judy Ditmer. Judy is a professional turner and the proprietor of Heartwoods in Tipp City, Ohio. She developed a line of small, simple-to-make boxes to use her scraps. She often turns dozens of them in a single day!

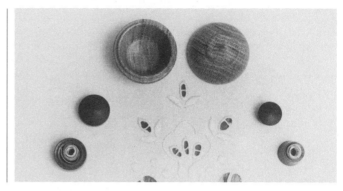

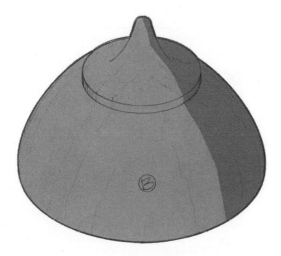

EXPLODED VIEW

Materials List

FINISHED DIMENSIONS

PARTS

A. Box   ³⁄₈″ to 2″ dia. x ³⁄₈″ to 2″

B. Lid   ³⁄₈″ to 2″ dia. x ³⁄₈″ to 2″

1

Select the stock and turn it to the rough dimensions. To make this project, you can use almost any small scrap of hardwood, as long as it's large enough to mount on your lathe. The harder and denser the wood, the better it will work. Softwood tends to splinter and chip when you try to turn fine detail.

Mount the wood on your lathe and spindle-turn a cylinder that's about ¼″ larger than the finished diameter you want the box to be. The cylinder should be at least 2″ long, but no longer than 5½″.

Turn a tenon on each end of the cylinder. Each tenon should be about ¾″ long (slightly longer for larger boxes) and no more than ½″ in diameter. (See Figure 1.)

Cut the cylinder in two parts with a band saw or coping saw, making a lid blank and a box blank. Each blank should have a tenon on one end. (See Figure 2.)

1/Turn a cylinder slightly larger than the finished diameter of the box. Make a tenon on each end of the cylinder.

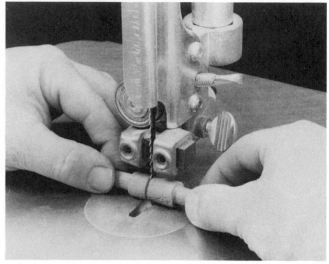

2/Cut the turned cylinder apart, making two pieces — a box blank and a lid blank. Each blank must have a tenon.

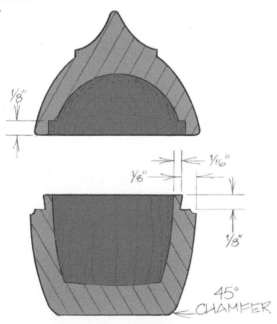

⅛″

⅛″ 1/16″

⅛″

45° CHAMFER

**SECTION VIEW
SAMPLE BOX**

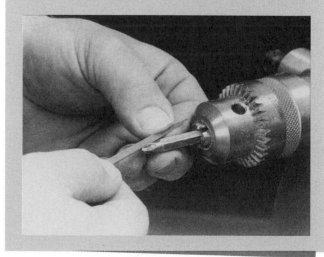

TRY THIS! To help turn small spindles, make a drive center from the tip and shaft of an old #2 Phillips screwdriver. (Larger drive centers sometimes get in the way.) Sharpen the tip with a triangular file so it will penetrate the wood easily.

2 **Turn the inside of the lid.** Remove the drive center and tailstock from your lathe and mount a lathe chuck on the drive shaft. The chuck shown in all subsequent photos has four jaws, but you can also use a three-jawed chuck or even a drill chuck. Most tool manufacturers offer these as accessories for their lathes.

Clamp the tenon of the lid blank in the jaws of the chuck. "Face" the bottom end of the blank — cut it flat with a chisel. (See Figure 3.) Then hollow out the inside of the lid and cut a ledge around the inside circumference. (See Figures 4 and 5.)

When you have finished cutting, apply a wax finish to the inside of the lid. Put a small amount of paste wax on a rag or fine steel wool and hold it against the spinning blank. (See Figure 6.) Wax makes an excellent finish for small lathe projects. You can use any kind of furniture wax, but most turners prefer a blend of carnauba and other natural waxes.

3/Face the end of the blank, cutting it flat. Your chisel must be very sharp to get a smooth cut.

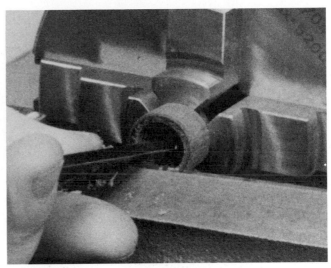

4/Hollow out the inside of the lid. Don't cut too close to the outside of the blank — remember to leave yourself some extra stock so you can turn the outside shape later. (The amount you leave will depend on the shape you want to turn.)

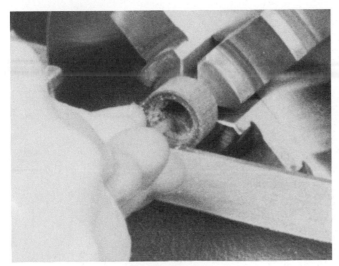

5/After you have hollowed out the lid, use a square or skew chisel to cut a ledge around the inside circumference. Later, you'll fit the lip of the box to this ledge.

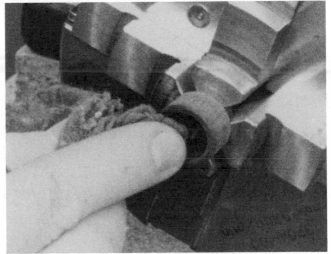

6/Apply paste wax to the inside of the lid while it turns on the lathe. This technique allows you to finish the parts of the box as you turn them.

3 Turn the lip on the box.

Remove the lid from the lathe chuck and mount the box blank. Face the box blank as you did the lid.

Measure the inside of the lid with a pair of calipers, and transfer these measurements to the faced surface of the box blank. (See Figures 7 and 8.) Turn a lip on the top of the box, using a skew chisel, and *undercut* the outside of the lip slightly, as shown in the *Box Lip*

Detail. (This undercut helps to create a tight fit — the box and the lid will seem to snap together when the lip is the proper diameter.) Stop cutting just before you get to the lines that mark the inside diameter of the lid. Check to see if the lid will fit. (See Figures 9 and 10.) If it won't, cut a little more and check again. Continue until you get a good fit. The lid should be snug, but not too tight.

7/Measure the inside diameter of the ledge in the lid. Use a pair of **steel** inside/outside calipers if you have them. These will allow you to transfer the measurement to the box blank quickly and easily.

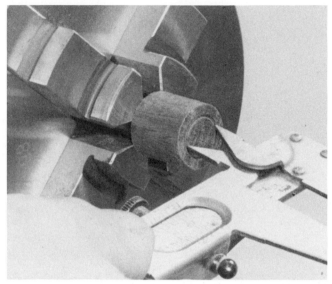

8/Position the sharp tips of the calipers on the lathe tool rest, in front of the box blank. Center them by eye. With the lathe spinning, push the tips forward so they lightly score the end of the blank. Use this score as a guide when you cut the box lip.

9/Make the box lip with a skew chisel, and undercut it slightly. Stop cutting just before you reach the line that marks the inside circumference of the lid.

10/Test fit the lid to the box lip. **Don't force it!** The fit should be snug, but not too tight. If the lid won't fit, remove a little more stock and try again. Continue until you get a good fit.

Warning: Don't force the lid onto the box lip. If the fit is too tight, the lid may split. A tight fit may also cause the sides of the box to collapse when you turn them. (See Figure 11.)

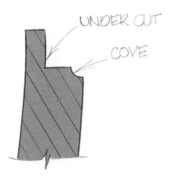

UNDER CUT

COVE

BOX LIP DETAIL

11/If the lid is too tight, it may split or the sides of the box may collapse. You may ruin a few boxes before you find out how to fit the lids just right.

4 **Turn the shape of the box and lid.** Cut the tenon off the lid, then press the lid onto the box. Turn the outside shape of both the box and the lid. (See Figure 12.) Make very light cuts, so the lid won't slip as you turn it. If the lid does begin to slip, remove it from the box and wet the lip slightly. Quickly replace the lid and hold it in place for a moment. The wood will swell, making the fit tighter.

After turning the shape of the box, sand it smooth and apply a wax finish. (See Figure 13.)

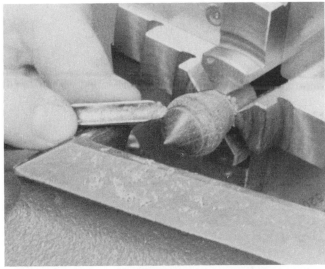

12/With the lid in place, turn the shape of the box and lid. Be careful not to cut the wall of the lid too thin — it will split. (The proper wall thickness for each box and lid will depend on the size and the kind of wood used. Experience will tell you when a box or lid is getting too thin.)

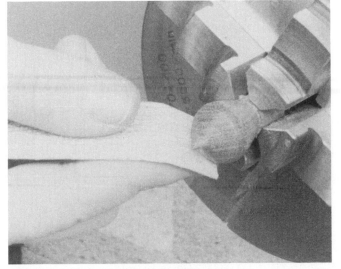

13/Sand the outside shape of the box and lid smooth, then apply a paste wax finish. Be careful that the lid doesn't heat up as you sand — this may cause it to crack.

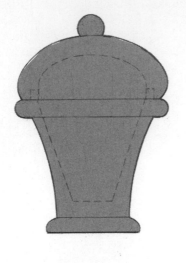

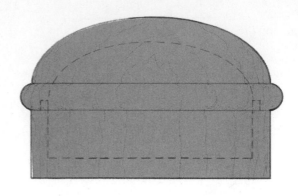

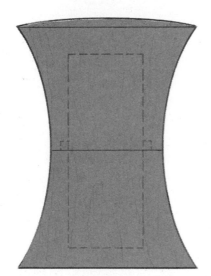

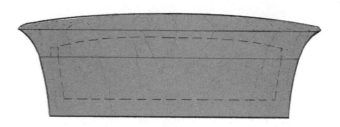

NOTE: CREATE A LIP, LEDGE OR BULGE ON EACH LID TO USE AS A HANDHOLD.

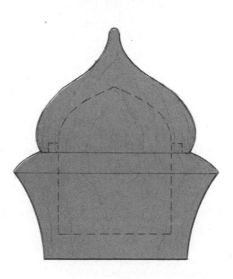

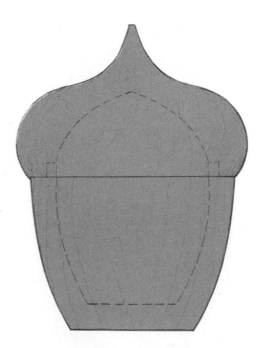

SAMPLE BOX SHAPES

5

Turn the inside of the box. Remove the lid from the box, and cut a cove in the edge, as shown in the *Box Lip Detail*. (See Figure 14.) As the wood expands and contracts with changes in humidity, the lid will change shape slightly. If you leave the box and lid surfaces flush where they join, the lid may look and feel mismatched — too big in some spots and too small in others. The tiny cove hides this and makes the lid look perfectly matched at all times.

After cutting the cove, hollow out the inside of the box. (See Figure 15.) Apply a wax finish to the inside.

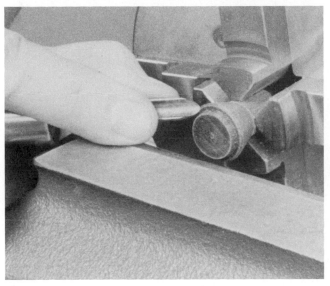

14/Cut a cove in the edge of the box, just below the lip. This cove helps disguise the normal wood movement and makes it difficult to detect slight changes in the shape of the lid.

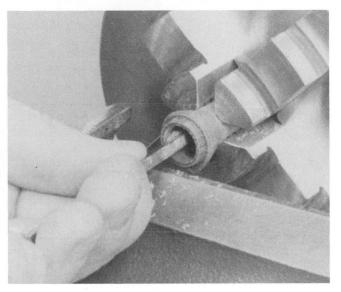

15/Hollow out the inside of the box in the same manner you did the lid, then apply a wax finish.

6

Face the bottom of the box. Remove the box from the chuck. Cut the tenon off, using a band saw or coping saw. Wrap the box in a thin strip of leather and *carefully* clamp it in the chuck so the bottom end faces out. Face the bottom of the box with a square or skew chisel, then apply paste wax. (See Figure 16.) Finally, remove the box from the chuck, unwrap it from the leather, and press the lid in place.

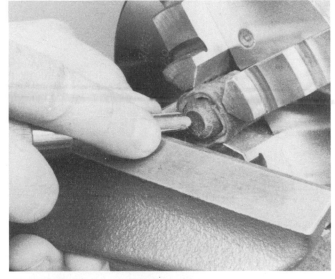

16/Cut the tenon off the box, wrap the box in leather to protect the wood, and clamp it in the chuck. Be careful when you tighten the chuck — you don't want to collapse the sides. Face the bottom of the box.

Step-by-Step: Making a Wooden Lathe Chuck

If you don't have a metal three-jaw or four-jaw chuck for your lathe, you can *turn* one from wood. A shop-made wooden chuck holds stock in much the same manner as a metal chuck, and offers two advantages: It will not mar the wood, nor will it crush it as easily as a metal chuck. However, it also has two limitations.

First, the wooden "jaws" aren't infinitely adjustable like their metal counterparts. You must make the tenons on the turning stock to fit the chuck. For some projects, such as the Turned Boxes, you must make several chucks with different inside diameters.

Second, a wooden chuck will not hold large stock as stable or as securely as a metal one. A wooden chuck will serve well for small projects (such as the Turned Boxes), but if you want to turn anything very large or heavy, invest in a metal chuck.

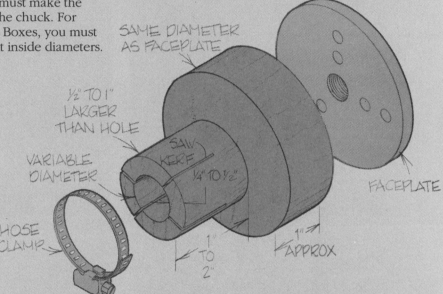

SAME DIAMETER AS FACEPLATE

½" TO 1" LARGER THAN HOLE

VARIABLE DIAMETER

SAW KERF

¼" TO ½"

HOSE CLAMP

FACEPLATE

1" TO 2"

1" APPROX

EXPLODED VIEW

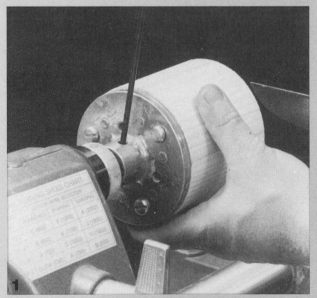

1

To make a wooden lathe chuck, first cut a blank the same diameter as your faceplate and 2"–3" long. Mount the blank on the faceplate, then mount the faceplate on the lathe.

2

Turn the lathe on low speed and mark the precise center, or **turning axis,** of the blank with a pencil or awl. You know you've located the center when you can put the point of a pencil (or awl) on the turning blank and it doesn't wiggle.

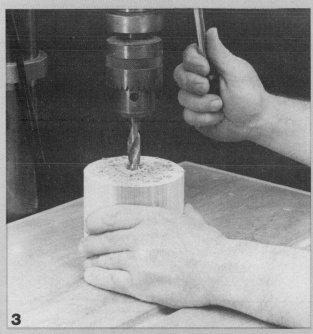

Remove the faceplate from the lathe and the blank from the faceplate. Drill a hole through the center of the blank. The diameter of this hole must be no smaller than 1/2", and no larger than the diameter of the blank minus 1".

Replace the blank and the faceplate on the lathe. Turn a cylinder on the end of the blank 1"–2" long. The diameter of this cylinder should be 1/2"–1" larger than the diameter of the hole.

Make the jaws of the chuck by cutting several kerfs with a dovetail saw or back saw across the diameter of the cylinder. A small chuck (with a cylinder under 1 1/2" in diameter) needs only two kerf cuts, creating four jaws. Larger chucks require more kerfs.

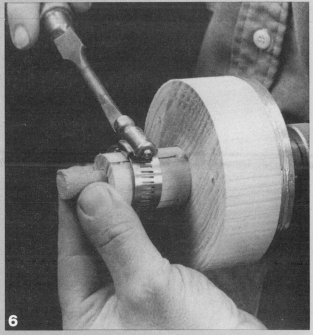

To mount turning stock in the chuck, first turn a tenon on the stock to the same diameter as the hole in the chuck. Slip a hose clamp over the jaws, insert the tenon in the hole, then tighten the clamp.

Christmas Crèche

Legend tells us that in 1223, St. Francis of Assisi preached the story of the nativity to the common people of the Italian countryside. To better illustrate the humble circumstances of the Christ Child's birth, he placed a carved figure of a baby in a small feeding trough or *crèche*. Italian peasants were soon carving their own figurines and using them to tell the story of Christmas to their children.

This practice spread throughout Europe, and by the sixteenth century whole *towns* were employed year-round in carving nativity scenes. What started as a simple wooden figure had expanded to become an entire cast of characters — the holy family, angels, oxen, sheep, shepherds, innkeepers, dogs, kings, camels, and on and on. Some medieval nativity displays evolved to include thousands of figurines, as new ones were added each year. The setting for this scene — the miniature stable and its surrounding landscape in which these characters were arranged — became known as a *Christmas crèche*.

Doug Crowell of Versailles, Ohio, designed this crèche and made one for each of his children. It's scaled to provide a setting for the 5″ and 6″ nativity figurines sold in many gift shops. In a tradition that goes back hundreds of years, Doug and his family add one new figure to their crèche each Christmas.

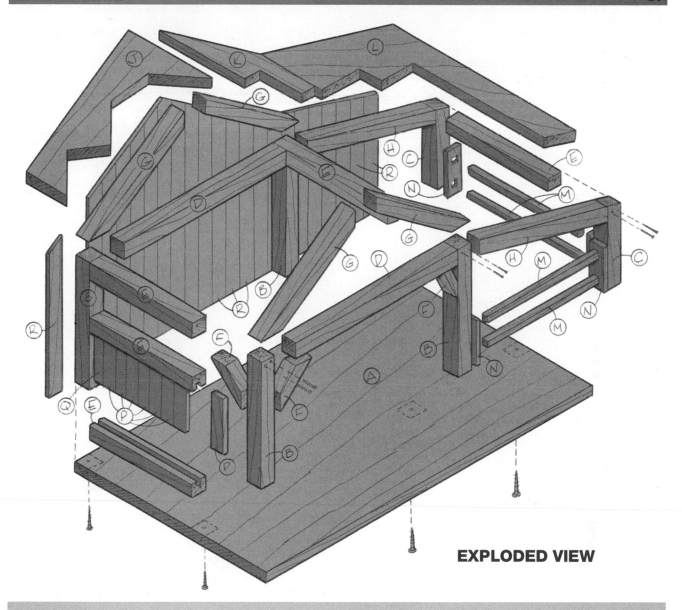

EXPLODED VIEW

Materials List

FINISHED DIMENSIONS

PARTS

A.	Base	1/2″ x 12″ x 19¼″
B.	Main posts (4)	3/4″ x 3/4″ x 6½″
C.	Shed posts (2)	3/4″ x 3/4″ x 4⅛″
D.	Front/back beams (2)	3/4″ x 3/4″ x 10½″
E.	Side beams (5)	3/4″ x 3/4″ x 6½″
F.	Braces (4)	3/4″ x 3/4″ x 3″
G.	Main rafters (4)	3/4″ x 3/4″ x 7⅜″
H.	Shed rafters (2)	3/4″ x 3/4″ x 7³⁄₁₆″
J.	Loft roof panel	3/8″ x 9¼″ x 8¹³⁄₁₆″
K.	Middle roof panel	3/8″ x 9¼″ x 7⁹⁄₁₆″
L.	Right roof panel	3/8″ x 9¼″ x 8¹⁵⁄₁₆″
M.	Rails (4)	3/8″ x 3/8″ x 6½″
N.	Rail keepers (4)	1/8″ x 3/4″ x 2½″
P.	Side boards (8)	1/8″ x 3/4″ x 3″
Q.	Narrow side board	1/8″ x 1/2″ x 3″
R.	Back boards (total)	1/8″ x 3/4″ x 240″

HARDWARE

#8 x 1¼″ Flathead wood screws (6)
4d Finishing nails (24–36)
3/4″ Wire brads (50–60)
1″ Wire brads (24–36)

1

Select the stock and cut the parts to size. To build this project, you need about 6 board feet of 4/4 (four-quarters) stock. You can use almost any wood — most of the pieces are small enough that you can make them from scraps, and you can paint the completed crèche to hide the different types of wood grain. The crèche shown is made from old, weathered barn siding. This gives it a rustic look.

When you have selected the wood, glue up the stock needed to make the base and the roof panels. Cut the parts to the sizes shown in the materials list, except those parts with one or more mitered ends — the braces, rafters, shed posts, and roof panels. Cut these about 1″ longer than specified. Cut the back board stock to the proper thickness and width, but don't cut the individual boards to length yet.

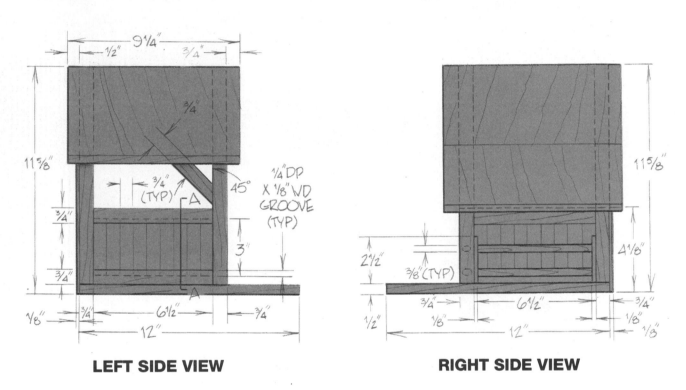

LEFT SIDE VIEW   **RIGHT SIDE VIEW**

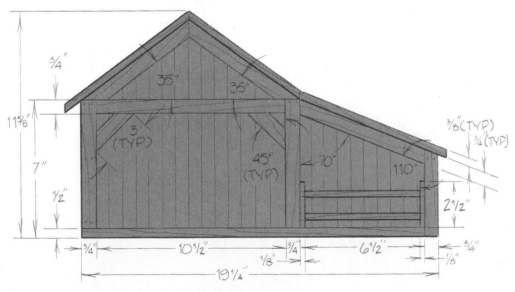

FRONT VIEW

2

Miter the frame parts. The braces, rafters, and shed posts are mitered on one or both ends. As you cut these, lay them flat on your workbench, butting the adjoining ends to test the fit. (See Figure 1.) If a part doesn't fit, adjust the length or the miter angle slightly.

Start by mitering the ends of the braces at 45°, as shown in the *Front View*. Lay two of the main posts and the front beam on the bench in the same configuration that you'll later assemble them. Lay the braces in place.

Miter the ends of the main rafters at 55° and 35° as shown in the *Main Rafter and Roof Panel Layout*. Lay two rafters in place above the posts and beam. Miter the top ends of the shed posts and both ends of the shed rafters at 70°. Lay one of each beside the right main post. Check the fit of all the miter joints.

1/To make sure that all the frame parts fit properly, lay them out on a flat surface as you cut them.

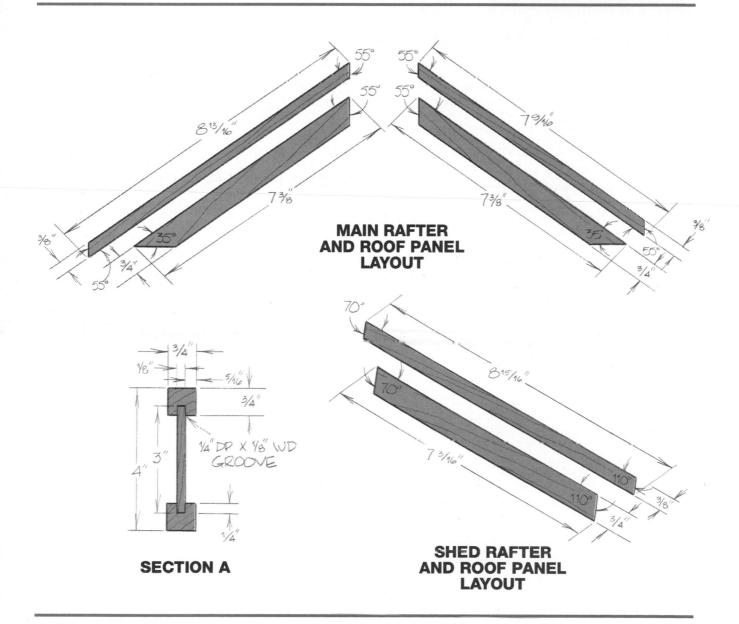

MAIN RAFTER AND ROOF PANEL LAYOUT

SECTION A

SHED RAFTER AND ROOF PANEL LAYOUT

3

Cut grooves in the beams for the side boards. The side boards rest in two ⅛"-wide, ¼"-deep grooves in two beams. Cut these grooves on a table saw, using a blade that cuts a ⅛"-wide kerf.

4

Assemble the frame. As you assemble the parts of the crèche, don't bother to sand them. Leave the saw marks, so the completed project will appear rough-hewn.

Glue the main posts, front beams, and back beams together to make two U-shaped assemblies. Let the glue dry, then add two braces to the front assembly. Again, let the glue dry and add the main rafters. Also glue the shed rafters to the shed posts.

Glue the ends of the side boards in the two grooves in the side beams. Let the glue dry, then sand the ends of the assembly clean and flush. Glue the side board assembly and two beams between the two main post assemblies. Reinforce the post-to-beam joints with 4d finishing nails. Glue braces to the front posts and beams.

Glue a beam between the two shed post assemblies. Once again, reinforce the joints with finishing nails.

Glue the main post assembly to the base and reinforce it with #8 x 1¼" flathead wood screws. Drive the screws up through the base and into the ends of the posts. Countersink the heads of the screws flush with the surface of the base.

Glue the shed post assembly to the main post assembly and the base. Again, secure the posts to the base with screws.

TRY THIS! When assembling the frame, use masking tape to keep the parts together while the glue dries. This tape is slightly elastic. If you wrap each joint tightly, the tape will provide enough pressure to get a strong glue bond.

5

Attach the back boards. Start by cutting the left-most back board slightly longer than needed. Lay it in place with the bottom end flush with the base. Mark the top end, cut the board to length, and glue it in place. Repeat for all the back boards, until you have completely covered the back of the crèche. You may have to trim the last, right-most back board to the proper width, as well as cut it to length. When the glue has dried, lightly sand the top ends of the back boards flush with the rafters.

6

Attach the roof panels. Bevel *both* ends of the middle roof panel at 55° and glue it in place. Reinforce it with 1″ wire brads. Bevel both ends of the left panel at 55° and the right panel at 70°. Glue the panels to the frame and reinforce them with brads.

7

Reinforce the back boards. After you attach the roof panels, the structure will be strong enough for you to secure the back boards to the rafters and base. Drive two ³/₄″ wire brads through each back board, one near the top and the other near the bottom.

8

Attach the rails. The rails are held in place with thin "keepers." Drill two ³/₈″-diameter holes through each keeper, then square these holes with a chisel, as shown in the *Rail Keeper Layout*. (See Figure 2.)
Insert the rails in the keeper holes. Then glue the keepers to the posts.

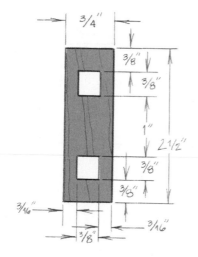

RAIL KEEPER LAYOUT

2/Square the holes in the rail keepers so the rails will fit. Use a chisel with a tip that's ¹/₄″ wide or less. A mortising chisel works best.

9

Finish the crèche. Sand the joints clean, then apply stain, paint, or another finish to the completed project. After the finish dries, sand the edges, rounding them over and partly wearing away the coating. This will help to make the stable look older. If you wish, *lightly* beat the project with a bunch of old keys on a key ring. This will put a number of small nicks and dents in the wood surface, aging it even more.

Letter Box

Do you need a container in your office to help separate incoming and outgoing letters? Or to sort the bills coming due from those that can wait a while? Or to divide the junk from the good stuff? This country-style letter box will help you organize your mail any way you want.

You can also use it in other rooms. Hang it in the kitchen to organize recipes, receipts, and coupons. Place it in the dining room to hold napkins and silverware. In the bedroom or bathroom, use it to hold combs and brushes. This open-ended box will hold and organize dozens of small items. ✸

Materials List

FINISHED DIMENSIONS

PARTS

A. Back $\frac{1}{4}$" x 8" x 11"
B. Divider $\frac{1}{4}$" x $6\frac{1}{4}$" x 11"
C. Front $\frac{1}{4}$" x $5\frac{1}{8}$" x 11"
D. Sides (2) $\frac{1}{4}$" x 3" x 5"
E. Bottom $\frac{1}{4}$" x $2\frac{1}{16}$" x $10\frac{1}{2}$"

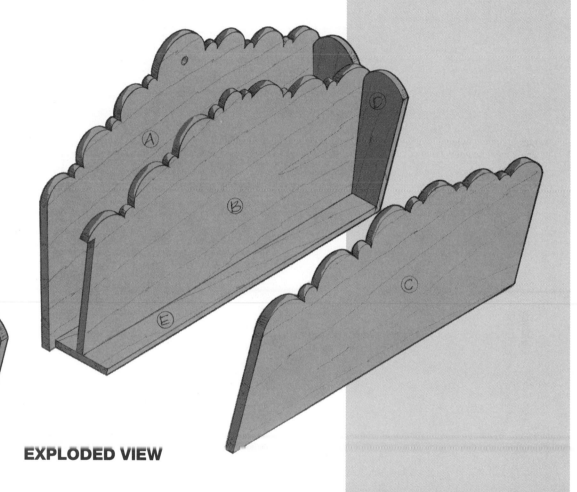

EXPLODED VIEW

HARDWARE

$\frac{3}{4}$" Wire brads (24–30)

1 Select the stock and cut it to size. To build this project, you need about 3 board feet of 4/4 (four-quarters) lumber. The parts are small enough to be made from scraps, and if you paint the completed letter box, you can use several kinds of wood. The paint will hide the mismatched stock.

When you have selected the wood, resaw and plane it to ¼″ thick. Cut the bottom to size, beveling the front edge at 15°. Cut the sides about ¼″ wider and longer than specified in the Materials List. Cut the front, back, and divider to the proper length, but make them ¼″ wider than specified.

2 Cut the shapes needed. Enlarge the *Front Pattern*, *Back Pattern*, and *Divider Pattern*, and trace them on the stock. Stack the side pieces face to face and tape them together so you can cut them both

at once. Lay out the shape of the sides on the top piece, as shown in the *Side Layout*.

Cut the shapes with a band saw or scroll saw. Sand the sawed edges smooth.

TRY THIS! This is a great project to mass-produce for gifts. You can make the parts for a dozen or more letter boxes all at once, in the time it takes to make them for one. When making a part, stack several boards face to face, sticking them together with double-faced carpet tape. Saw the shape and sand the edges with the pieces stacked. Then take the stack apart and discard the tape — you'll have several identical parts.

3 Drill a hole in the back. The letter box will either sit on a surface or hang on a wall. If you want to have the option of hanging it, drill a ¼″-

diameter hole through the back as shown in the *Front View* and *Back Pattern*.

4 Assemble the parts. Finish sand the parts, being careful not to round over any adjoining edges. Dry assemble the parts with masking tape — *don't* glue them — to check the fit. They don't have to fit perfectly; you can easily make the necessary adjustments during the final assembly.

When you're satisfied the parts fit reasonably well, begin the final assembly. First, attach the sides to the

bottom with glue and brads. Let the glue dry, then sand the edges flush on a belt sander or disk sander. This will ensure that the front and back fit perfectly.

Attach the front and back with glue and brads. Finally, put the divider in place. File or sand the divider edges as needed to get a good fit, then secure it with glue and brads. Let the glue dry completely and sand all joints clean and flush.

5

Finish the letter box. Set the heads of the brads slightly below the surface of the wood and cover them with putty. Do any necessary touch-up sand-ing, then apply paint, stain, or a finish to the completed letter box.

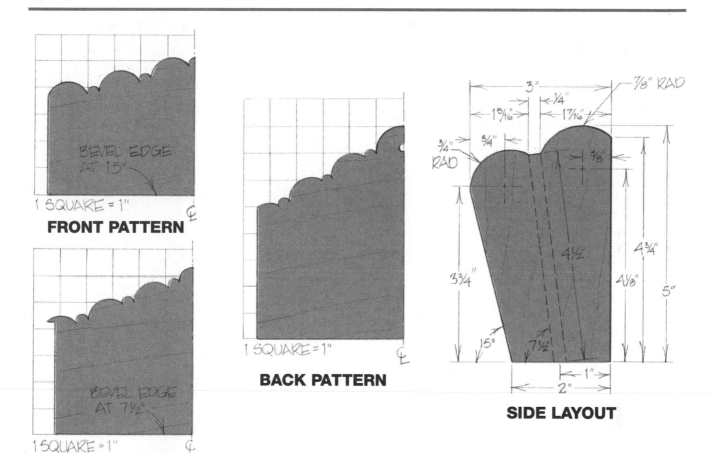

FRONT PATTERN

DIVIDER PATTERN

BACK PATTERN

SIDE LAYOUT

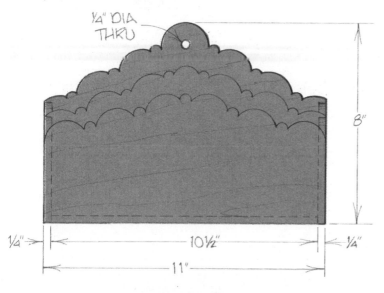

FRONT VIEW

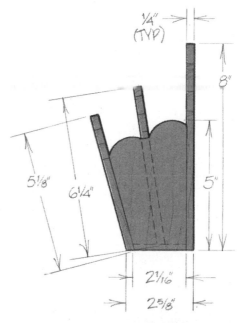

SIDE VIEW

Fireman's Ladder

For generations, this simple toy design has entertained both children and adults. Place the small, wooden man on the ladder with his feet hooked over the top rail. Let him go and he will climb down, tumbling from rung to rung. If you want, put two men on the ladder and watch them race to the bottom.

This folk toy goes by many different names. It has been called Jacob's ladder, tumblers, and ladder race, to list a few. This particular version is called the Fireman's Ladder. The men are painted to look like firemen, and the base is shaped like a fire engine. The ladder pulls apart and stores on the back of the engine, while the firemen sit in the seat. ●

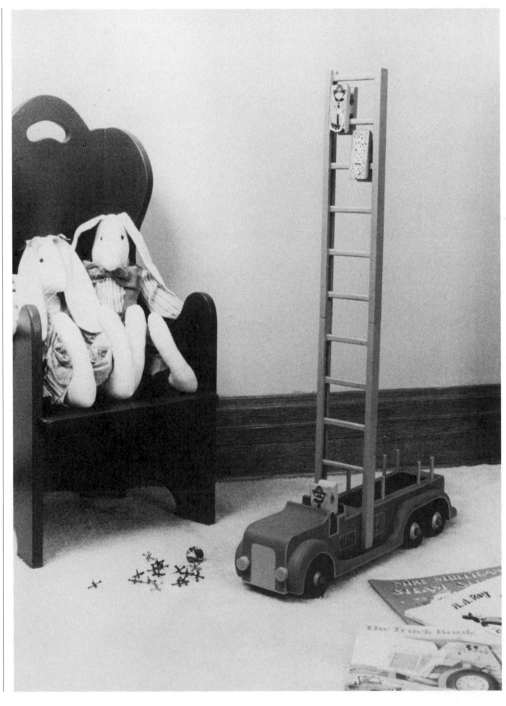

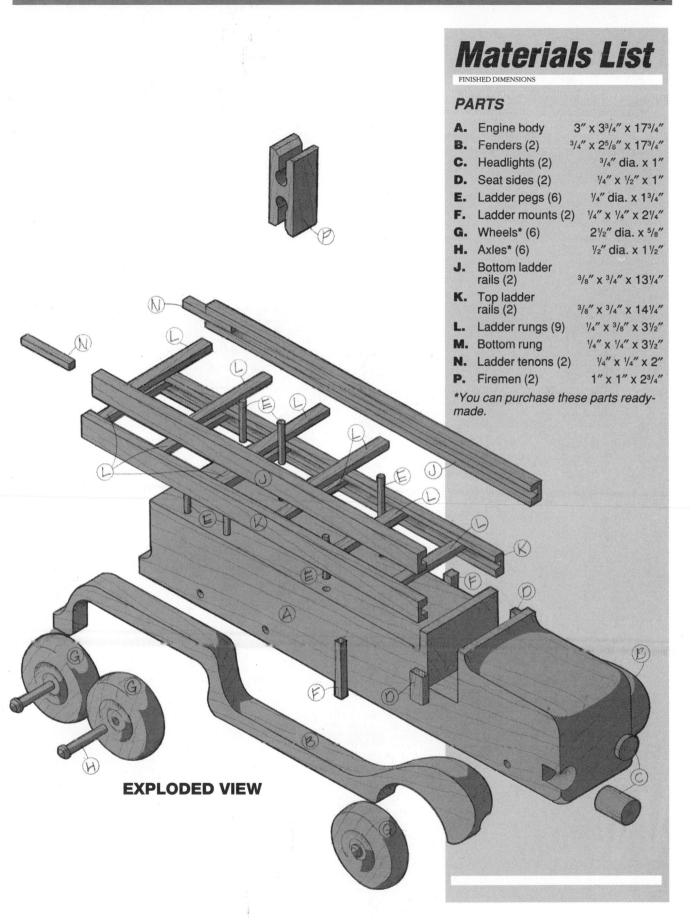

Materials List

FINISHED DIMENSIONS

PARTS

A.	Engine body	3″ x 3³/₄″ x 17³/₄″
B.	Fenders (2)	³/₄″ x 2⁵/₈″ x 17³/₄″
C.	Headlights (2)	³/₄″ dia. x 1″
D.	Seat sides (2)	¹/₄″ x ¹/₂″ x 1″
E.	Ladder pegs (6)	¹/₄″ dia. x 1³/₄″
F.	Ladder mounts (2)	¹/₄″ x ¹/₄″ x 2¹/₄″
G.	Wheels* (6)	2¹/₂″ dia. x ⁵/₈″
H.	Axles* (6)	¹/₂″ dia. x 1¹/₂″
J.	Bottom ladder rails (2)	³/₈″ x ³/₄″ x 13¹/₄″
K.	Top ladder rails (2)	³/₈″ x ³/₄″ x 14¹/₄″
L.	Ladder rungs (9)	¹/₄″ x ³/₈″ x 3¹/₂″
M.	Bottom rung	¹/₄″ x ¹/₄″ x 3¹/₂″
N.	Ladder tenons (2)	¹/₄″ x ¹/₄″ x 2″
P.	Firemen (2)	1″ x 1″ x 2³/₄″

You can purchase these parts ready-made.

EXPLODED VIEW

1

Select the stock and cut the parts to size. To make this project, you need about 4 board feet of 4/4 (four-quarters) lumber, a scrap of 5/4 (five-quarters) lumber, a 12″ length of ¼″-diameter dowel, and a 3″ length of ¾″-diameter dowel. So the toy will stand up to the abuse that children sometimes give their playthings, all of this stock should be clear hardwood — the harder, the better. The Fireman's Ladder shown is made from rock maple and birch.

Note: The materials estimate includes enough stock to turn your own wheels and axles. However, you may prefer to purchase these parts ready-made from a craft store or woodworking supplier. If so, you need only 3½″ board feet of 4/4 stock.

When you have selected the stock, plane all the 4/4 lumber to ¾″ thick. Glue up the stock needed to make the engine body. Then cut all the parts to the sizes given in the Materials List, except the wheels, axles, and ladder rails. If you're turning your own wheels and axles, cut these parts slightly larger to give yourself the extra stock needed to mount them on the lathe. Don't worry about the ladder rails right now; you'll make these later.

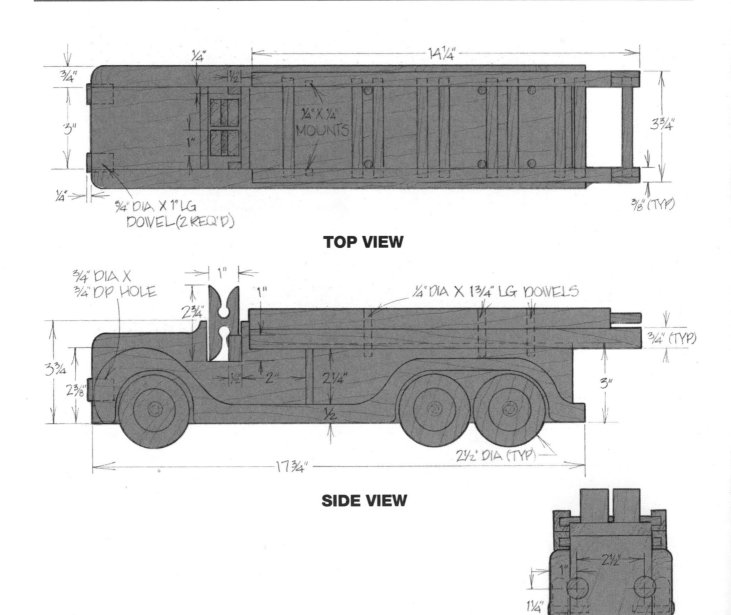

TOP VIEW

SIDE VIEW

FRONT VIEW

2

Cut the shapes of the engine and fenders. Stack the two fender parts face to face and stick them together with double-faced carpet tape. Make sure the edges and ends are flush. Enlarge the *Fender Pattern* and trace it on the top part. Also, lay out the engine body as shown in the *Engine Body Layout/Side View*.

Cut the shapes, using a band saw or scroll saw. Leave the fenders taped together and sand the sawed surfaces. Then take the fenders apart and discard the tape.

3

Drill the holes in the engine body. Lay out the location of the ladder pegs, as shown in the *Engine Body/Top View,* and the axles, as shown in the *Engine Body/Side View*. Drill ¼″-diameter, ½″-deep holes for the ladder pegs and ⁵⁄₁₆″-diameter, 1⅛″-deep holes for the axles.

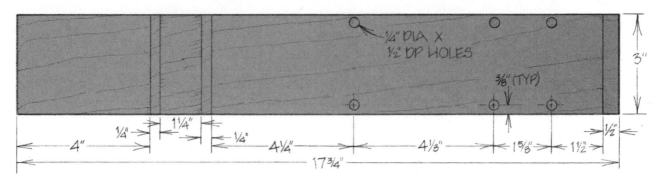

TOP VIEW

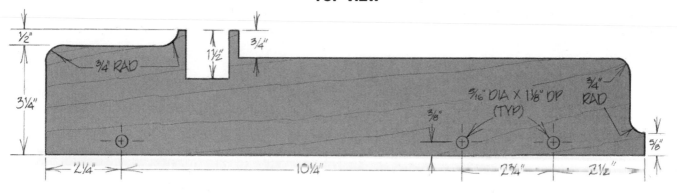

SIDE VIEW

ENGINE BODY LAYOUT

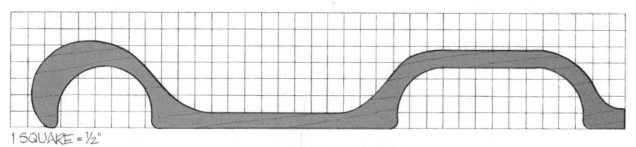

FENDER PATTERN

4 Assemble the engine.

Finish sand the engine body, fenders, seat sides, ladder pegs, and headlights. Glue the fenders and seat sides to the body, then let the glue dry completely. Round over the fenders, then sand the glue joints clean and flush. (See Figure 1.)

Drill two ¾″-diameter, ¾″-deep holes in the front end of the engine body and fenders, as shown in the *Front View*. Glue the headlights in these holes. Also, glue the ladder pegs in the holes in the top of the engine body.

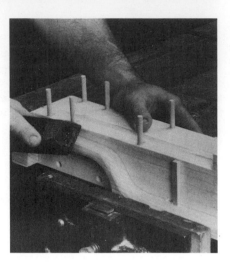

1/Round over the top outside edges of the fenders with a rasp, file, and sandpaper. They're much easier to round when attached to the engine body.

5 Make the ladders.

To make the ladder rails, select a piece of ¾″-thick stock, 2″–4″ long, and at least 15″ long, with clear, straight grain. Joint both edges, and cut a ¼″-wide, ¼″-deep groove in the center of each edge. Then rip a ⅜″-thick rail from each edge. Repeat, so you have four rails. (See Figures 2 and 3.)

Cut the rails to length and finish sand both the rails and the rungs. Carefully measure the locations of the rails, as shown in the *Top Ladder Layout* and *Bottom Ladder Layout*. Glue the rungs in the rail grooves. Note that the bottom rung on the bottom ladder is just ¼″ wide, while the others are ⅜″.

*2/To make the ladder rails, **first** cut grooves in the edges of a large board.*

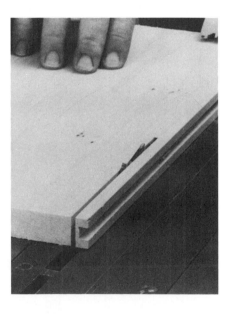

*3/**Then** rip the rails from the stock. If you try to cut the grooves after you rip the rails to size, the narrow rails may splinter or break.*

6 Fit and attach the ladder mounts and ladder tenons.

The 1″-long tenons on the bottom ladder fit into the grooves in the top ladder rails, holding the two together. The ladder slips over the mounts on the sides of the fire engine.

Before gluing the tenons and mounts in place, make sure they fit the grooves properly. Each piece should be snug in its respective groove, with no slop. But it shouldn't be so tight that you have to force it. If a tenon or mount is too tight, remove a little stock from the surfaces with sandpaper. If it's too loose, make a new part.

When the tenons and mounts fit properly, glue them in place.

7

Make the firemen. Lay out the holes and slots in the fireman stock, as shown in the *Fireman Layout*. Drill 7/16"-diameter holes through the stock, then open up each hole by cutting a 5/16"-wide slot from the end of the stock. Use a band saw, scroll saw, or table saw to make these slots. Chamfer the open ends of the slots at 45°. Sand the firemen, slightly rounding all corners.

Note: The width of the slots is *critical*. They must be *precisely* 5/16" wide.

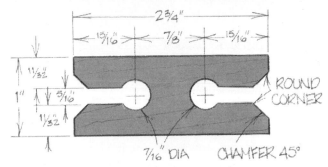

FIREMAN LAYOUT

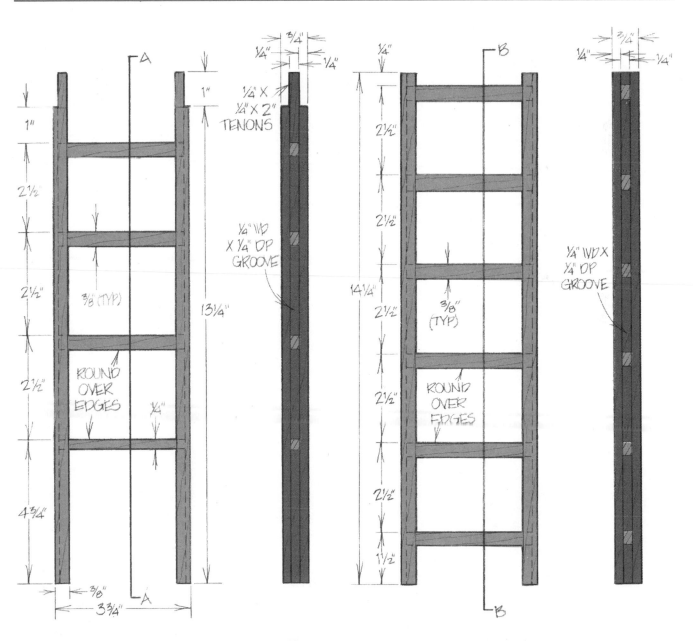

BOTTOM LADDER LAYOUT   **SECTION A**   **TOP LADDER LAYOUT**   **SECTION B**

8

Round the ladder rungs. Slightly round the edges of the ladder rungs, using a file and sandpaper. Fit the top and bottom ladders together, then mount the ladder assembly vertically on the fire engine mounts.

Place a fireman at the top of the ladder and fit the top rung into one of the slots. Let him go. He should tumble upside down, slide down onto the next rung, tumble right side up, slide down another rung, and repeat until he reaches the bottom of the ladder. To remove the fireman, turn it so the slot is horizontal and slide him off the bottom rung. If the fireman hangs up on one of the rungs or won't slide off the bottom rung, file the edges of the rung until he operates properly. Repeat for the other fireman, to make sure he works, too.

9

Make the wheels and axles (optional). If you choose to make your own wheels and axles, turn them on a lathe. Duplicate the shapes shown in the *Wheel Profile* and *Axle Layout*.

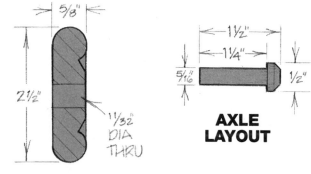

WHEEL PROFILE

AXLE LAYOUT

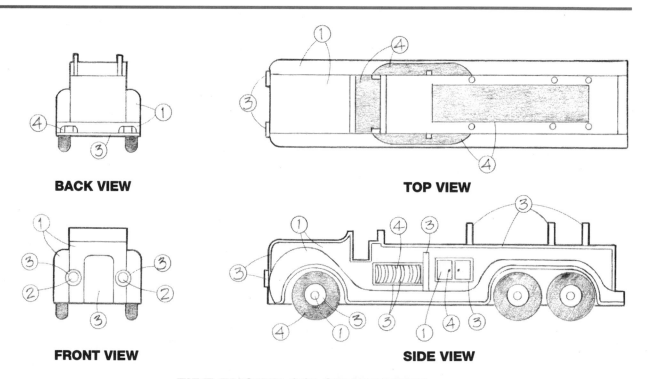

BACK VIEW

TOP VIEW

FRONT VIEW

SIDE VIEW

FIRE ENGINE COLOR PATTERN

COLOR CHART			
① RED		④ BLACK	
② YELLOW		⑤ BLUE	
③ SILVER		⑥ WHITE	

10

Paint the fire engine, wheels, axles, ladders, and firemen. Do any necessary touch-up sanding on the parts and assemblies you've made so far. Paint the fire engine, wheels, axles, and ladders, as shown in the *Fire Engine Color Pattern*. When painting the axles, be careful not to get any paint on the axle shaft.

Before painting the firemen, decide what kind of firemen to make. The patterns show a fireman with a hose, another with an axe, and a dalmatian. Choose any two, then color them following the "paint by numbers" code on the *Fireman with Hose Pattern, Fireman with Axe Pattern,* or *Dalmatian Pattern*. Don't get any paint into the holes and slots.

11

Mount the wheels, ladders, and firemen on the fire engine. When the paint dries, put a little wax on each axle near the knob. This will help the wheels turn smoothly. Insert an axle through each wheel and glue the small end of the axle into one

of the $5/16''$-diameter holes in the fire engine body. Be careful not to get any glue on the wheels.

Finally, put the ladders on the back of the engine, placing them over the pegs. Set the firemen in the seat, side by side.

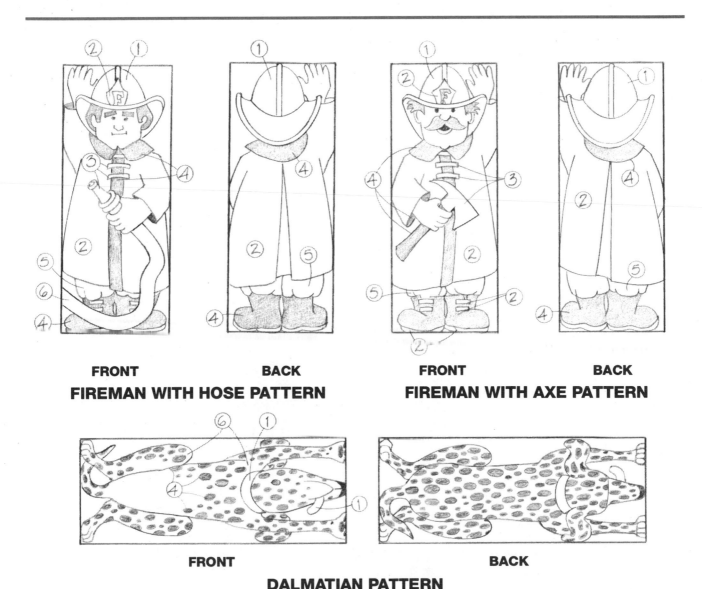

FRONT   **BACK**

FIREMAN WITH HOSE PATTERN

FRONT   **BACK**

FIREMAN WITH AXE PATTERN

FRONT   **BACK**

DALMATIAN PATTERN

Bathroom Cabinets

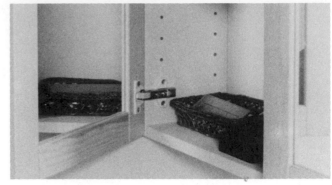

Most bathrooms come equipped with a small cabinet, barely 3″ deep and no bigger than a shaving mirror. This quickly fills up with toothpaste, shaving cream, hairbrushes, aspirin, and thousands of other toiletry tools and materials. Before long, it's impossible to open the door without half a dozen bottles of cold cures and skin lotions falling out into the sink.

If you need more cabinet space in your bathroom for these essentials, consider this easy-to-build cabinet system. It's just a row of boxes bolted together and hung on the wall. Each box has several adjustable shelves and a mirrored door.

There are several advantages to this system, besides being easy and inexpensive to build. Because the design is modular, you can make as many boxes as you need for your toiletries. The size of the boxes can be easily adjusted to fit your bathroom and you can add as many shelves as needed. If you make three or more boxes, you can adjust the mirrored doors to see three sides of your face at once.

Materials List

FINISHED DIMENSIONS

PARTS

A. Sides (2) $\frac{1}{2}''$ x (variable) x (variable)

B. Top/ bottom (2) $\frac{1}{2}''$ x (variable) x (variable)

C. Hanger $\frac{1}{2}''$ x $1\frac{3}{4}''$ x (variable)

D. Door stiles (2) $\frac{3}{4}''$ x $1\frac{3}{4}''$ x (variable)

E. Door rails (2) $\frac{3}{4}''$ x $1\frac{3}{4}''$ x (variable)

F. Adjustable shelves (1–5) $\frac{1}{2}''$ x (variable) x (variable)

EXPLODED VIEW

HARDWARE

$\frac{1}{8}''$ x (variable) x (variable) Mirrors (2)

Self-closing, full overlay European-style hinges and mounting screws (2)

Pin-style shelving supports (4–20)

#8 x $1\frac{1}{4}''$ Flathead wood screws (12)

#12 x $2\frac{1}{2}''$ Flathead wood screws (2)

$\frac{3}{16}''$ x $1\frac{1}{4}''$ Stove bolts, flat washers, and nuts (2)

1

Determine the size of the cabinets and how many to make. Measure the wall where you will hang the cabinets. Working with these measurements, decide the height of the cabinets — they should be somewhere between 20″ and 36″ tall. If you make the cabinets shorter, they may be too small to be useful. If you make them taller, you may not be able to reach the items on the top shelves easily.

Next, decide how wide each cabinet should be and how many to make. The width should be between 12″ and 20″. If you make them narrower, you may not be able to see your entire face in one of the mirrored doors. If they're wider, the doors may get in the way when you open them. Divide the length of the wall area by whole numbers until you get an answer between 12

and 20. For example, if you have a space 80″ long, you might divide 80 by 5 to get 16. Make five cabinets, each 16″ wide.

Finally, decide the depth of the cabinet. This depends partly on what's under the cabinets and how high they should be above these items. You don't want the cabinets to block you from seeing the faucet handle on the sink, or to make it difficult to reach a towel rack. The depth also depends on the width of the doors. If the doors are wide (16″–20″), you probably want to make the cabinets shallow (4″–5″). Otherwise, the doors will stick out past the bathroom sink when they're open. If the doors are narrower, you can make the cabinets deeper.

2

Select the stock and cut the parts to size. Once you've determined what size to make the cabinets and how many to make, calculate the dimensions of the various parts in the Materials List. Then figure how much wood you'll need.

Next, decide what materials to use. Since this project will be used in a bathroom, choose a close-grained wood such as cherry, maple, birch, or poplar. Close-grained woods absorb moisture more slowly than those

with open grains. If you plan to paint the cabinets, select an inexpensive wood. If you plan to finish them naturally, choose an attractive cabinet-grade hardwood. The cases of the cabinets shown were made from poplar and painted white. The door frames, however, were made from birch and finished with clear varnish.

When you have selected and purchased the materials, cut all the parts to the proper sizes.

3

Cut the grooves in the rails and stiles. The mirrors rest in ¼″-wide, ¼″-deep grooves in the door rails and stiles. Cut these grooves with a table-mounted router or dado cutter, using a fence to guide the stock over the cutter. (See Figure 1.)

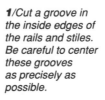
1/Cut a groove in the inside edges of the rails and stiles. Be careful to center these grooves as precisely as possible.

4

Cut the rabbets and tenons. The top and bottom of each cabinet rest in ½″-wide, ¼″-deep rabbets in the ends of the sides. The ends of the door rails have ¼″-thick, 1″-long tenons. Both of these can be cut with the same tools and similar setups.

Cut the rabbets with a table-mounted router or dado cutter, using a miter gauge to feed the stock across the bit or blade. Without changing the height of the cutter above the table, cut the tenons in the ends of the rails. Cut a practice tenon in a scrap first to check that it fits the grooves in the stiles. If necessary, adjust the height of the cutter *slightly*. Then cut the tenons in the good stock. Make each tenon in two passes — cut one side of the rail, turn it over, and cut the other. (See Figure 2.)

2/*When cutting the rabbets and the tenons, use a miter gauge to guide the stock over the cutter. Attach an extension to the gauge, then clamp a stop block to the extension. Use the stop block to stop the cut when the rabbet is the right width or the tenon is the right length.*

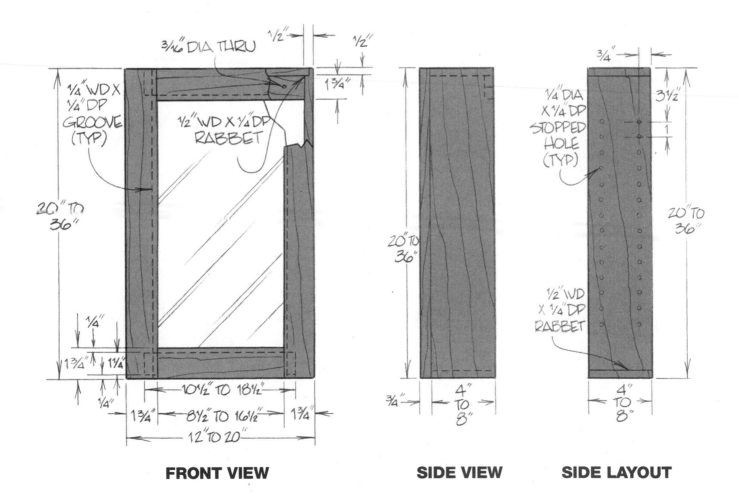

FRONT VIEW   **SIDE VIEW**   **SIDE LAYOUT**

5

Cut the mortises and haunches. The tenons on the ends of the rails fit in ¼"-wide, 1"-deep, 1¼"-long mortises in the stiles. Rough out these mortises by drilling a series of ¼"-diameter holes in the grooved edges of the stiles. Then square the sides and ends of the mortises with a chisel. (See Figures 3 and 4.)

The tenons are notched or "haunched" to fit in the mortises, as shown in the *Door Joinery Detail*. Cut these haunches with a band saw or dovetail saw. (See Figure 5.)

3/Rough out the mortises by drilling ¼"-diameter, 1"-deep holes to remove most of the waste. Clamp a fence to the drill press table to help position the stock under the bit.

4/Remove the remaining waste from the mortise and square it with a chisel. A mortising chisel works best for this chore.

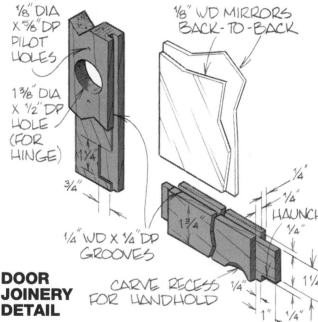

DOOR JOINERY DETAIL

⅛" DIA X ⅝" DP PILOT HOLES

1⅜" DIA X ½" DP HOLE (FOR HINGE)

1¼"

¾"

¼" WD X ¼" DP GROOVES

CARVE RECESS FOR HANDHOLD

⅛" WD MIRRORS BACK-TO-BACK

1¾"

¼"

¼"

HAUNCH

¼"

1¼"

¼"

1"

¼"

*5/To fit the tenon to the mortise, cut a notch or **haunch** in the outside corner.*

6

Drill holes in the sides. The adjustable shelves in the cabinet rest on pin supports. These pins fit into ¼"-diameter, ⅜"-deep holes in the sides. Mark the locations of these holes and drill them, as shown in the *Side Layout*.

7 Assemble the cabinet.

Assemble the cabinet. Finish sand all the parts you've made so far, then assemble the sides, top, bottom, and hanger with glue. Reinforce the glue joints with #8 x 1¼″ flathead wood screws. Countersink the screws so the heads are flush with the outside surface of the sides.

8 Assemble and fit the door.

Assemble and fit the door. Glue the rails and stiles together, inserting the tenons in the mortises. As you assemble the door parts, place the mirrors back to back and slide them into the grooves.

When the glue dries, mount the door on the cabinet using European-style hinges, such as those made by Blum. These allow the doors to swing open even when they are flush with one another.

European-style hinges aren't mortised into the door or the case in the normal manner; they're mounted in stopped holes. Using a Forstner bit or multispur bit, drill 1⅜″-diameter, ½″-deep holes in the inside face of the door stiles to hold the body of the hinge. Also, drill ⅛″-diameter, ⅝″-deep pilot holes for the mounting screws. (See Figures 6 and 7.) The positions of these holes vary with the make of the hinge — refer to the manufacturer's directions.

With a chisel, carve a shallow recess in the inside bottom edge of the door stile, just wide enough to hook two or three fingers in and pull the door open.

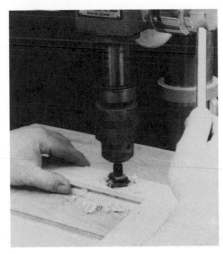

6/To mount a European-style cabinet hinge, drill a 1⅜″-diameter, ½″-deep hole in the door stile. The position of this hole varies from one manufacturer to another. Special bits are available.

7/Drill ⅛″-diameter, ⅝″-deep holes for the hinge mounting screws in the stile and the side. The positions of these holes may also vary. Several woodworking supply companies sell templates to locate these holes, or you can make your own.

9 Finish the cabinet.

Finish the cabinet. Remove the door from the cabinet and the hardware from the door. Do any necessary touch-up sanding and mask the mirrors with tape and newspaper. Apply paint or finish to the wooden parts. Be sure to use a waterproof finish, such as exterior latex paint or spar varnish.

10 Hang the cabinets.

Hang the cabinets. If you've made more than one cabinet, clamp them together side by side. Make sure the tops, bottoms, front edges, and back edges are flush. Drill two ³⁄₁₆″-diameter holes through the sides of each pair of adjoining cabinets, making one hole near the top and the other near the bottom. Then bolt the cabinets together with ³⁄₁₆″-diameter stove bolts, flat washers, and nuts.

Locate the studs in the bathroom wall. With a helper, hold the cabinets against the wall. Keep them in place with "dead men" — 2 x 4s cut to the right length to prop up the cabinets where you want them. Drill ³⁄₁₆″-diameter holes through the hangers in the back of the cabinets and into the studs. Secure the cabinets to the wall studs with #12 x 2½″ flathead wood screws.

Remove the dead men and replace the doors on the cabinets. Finally, install the shelving supports and the adjustable shelves.

Garden Stand

Just as you find small "occasional" tables useful around the house, stands are wonderfully versatile in the yard and garden. You can use them to hold potted plants, statuary, birdbaths, and other outdoor ornaments. They also work well as serving tables and stands for barbecue tools. The stand shown holds a sundial, but you can use it to hold or display almost any small or medium-sized item.

This design can be built to almost any size or height, depending on how you want to use it and what you want it to hold. You can make it portable or fasten it permanently in place. And it's extremely simple to build — you can make three or four of these stands in an afternoon. ✺

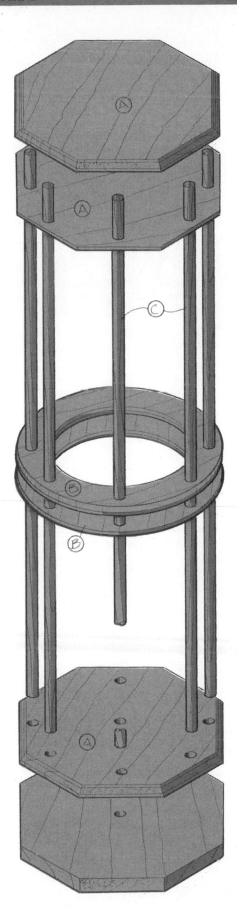

**EXPLODED
VIEW**

Materials List

FINISHED DIMENSIONS

PARTS

A. Tops/
bottoms (4) ³/₄″ x 11½″ x 11½″
B. Middle rings* (2) 11½″ dia. x ⁵/₈″
C. Dowels (8) ³/₄″ dia. x (variable)

*If the stand is less than 20″ high, you
may omit these rings.*

HARDWARE

4d Galvanized finishing nails (8)
½″ x 6″ Anchor bolt, washer, and nut
(optional)

1

Select the stock and cut it to size. To build this project, you need about 6 board feet of 4/4 (four-quarters) lumber and several ¾"-diameter dowels. Dowels come in 36" and 48" lengths. Decide how tall you want to make the stand, then calculate the number of dowels needed.

The stand can be built from almost any cabinet-grade wood, but mahogany, teak, redwood, cedar, and cypress will weather best. These woods have natural oils that make them rot-resistant. You can purchase ready-made mahogany dowels, but you'll have to turn your own if you use the other woods mentioned.

When you have determined the height of the stand and selected the stock, plane the stock. Then cut the parts to the sizes shown in the Materials List.

2

Drill holes in a top, a bottom, and the rings. Stack *one* of the tops, *one* of the bottoms, and *both* of the rings face to face. Hold the parts together with double-faced carpet tape. On the top part, mark the locations of the ¾"-diameter dowel holes, as shown in the *Top/Bottom Layout* and *Middle Ring Layout*.

Drill the holes through the entire stack. Mark the inside surface of one hole on all four parts. (Later, this will enable you to assemble the parts in the same orientation in which you drilled them.) Separate the parts and discard the tape.

TRY THIS! If you want to use the middle rings as a shelf, don't remove the inside. Leave them as disks. Another option is to cut them to the same octagonal shape as the tops and bottoms.

3

Cut the shapes of the parts. Stack all the tops and bottoms, sticking them together with double-faced tape. Lay out the octagonal shape of the tops and bottoms on the top piece in the stack, as shown in the *Top/Bottom Layout*. Do the same for the rings — stack the boards and mark the top piece.

Saw the octagonal shape with a band saw, table saw,

or radial arm saw. Cut the rings with a scroll saw or saber saw. To remove the waste inside the rings, first drill a ½"-diameter hole through the waste. Insert the blade of the saw through the hole and cut to the inside layout line. Cut around the line, removing the waste. Sand the sawed edges of both stacks, then separate the parts and discard the tape.

4

Shape the edges of the tops, a bottom, and the rings. Using a router or shaper, shape the circumference of *both* tops and *one* bottom.

The edge profile shown in *Section A* is a suggestion; you can cut any profile that suits your fancy. Leave the edge square on the bottom that you did *not* drill.

Shape the inside *and* outside circumference of the rings. Once again, the profile shown in *Section B* is a suggestion; you can cut any shape you wish.

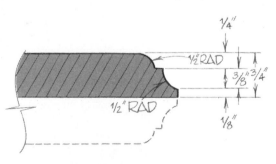

SECTION A

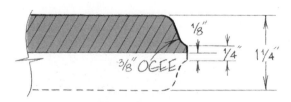

SECTION B

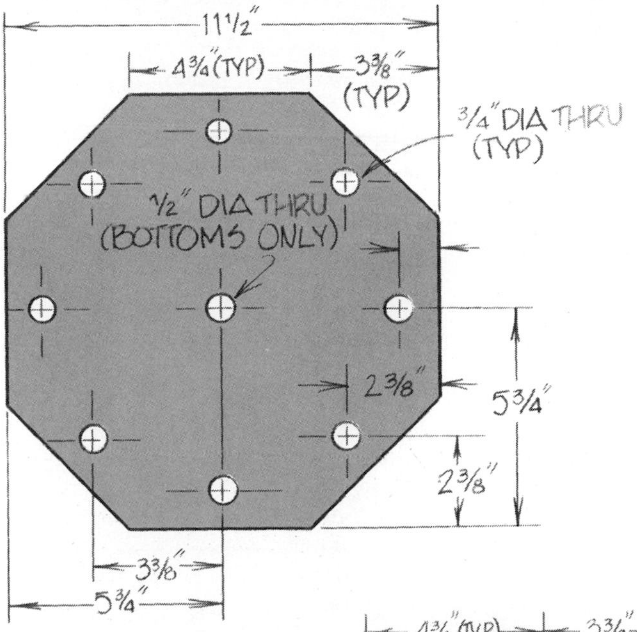
11½"
4¾" (TYP)
3⅜" (TYP)
¾" DIA THRU (TYP)
½" DIA THRU (BOTTOMS ONLY)
2⅜"
5¾"
2⅜"
3⅜"
5¾"

TOP/BOTTOM LAYOUT

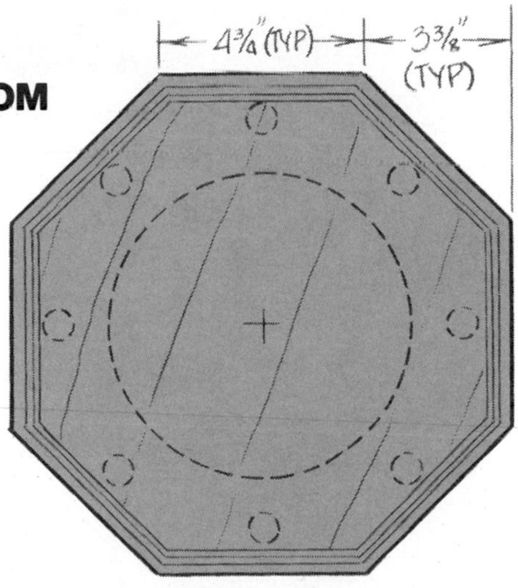
4¾" (TYP)
3⅜" (TYP)

TOP VIEW

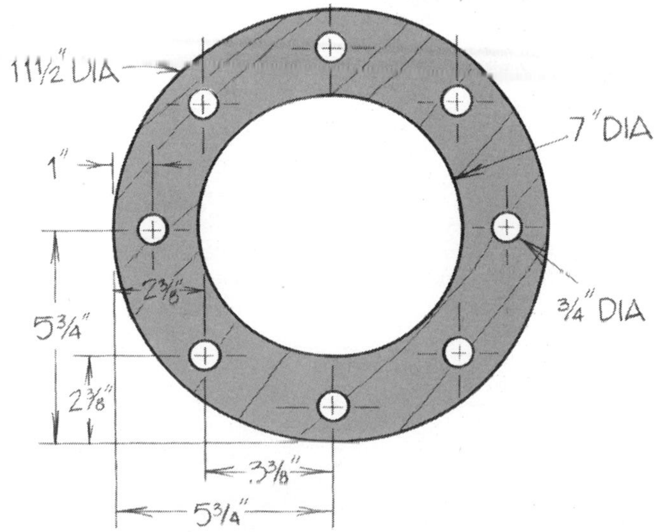
11½" DIA
7" DIA
1"
5¾"
2⅜"
2⅜"
¾" DIA
3⅜"
5¾"

MIDDLE RING LAYOUT

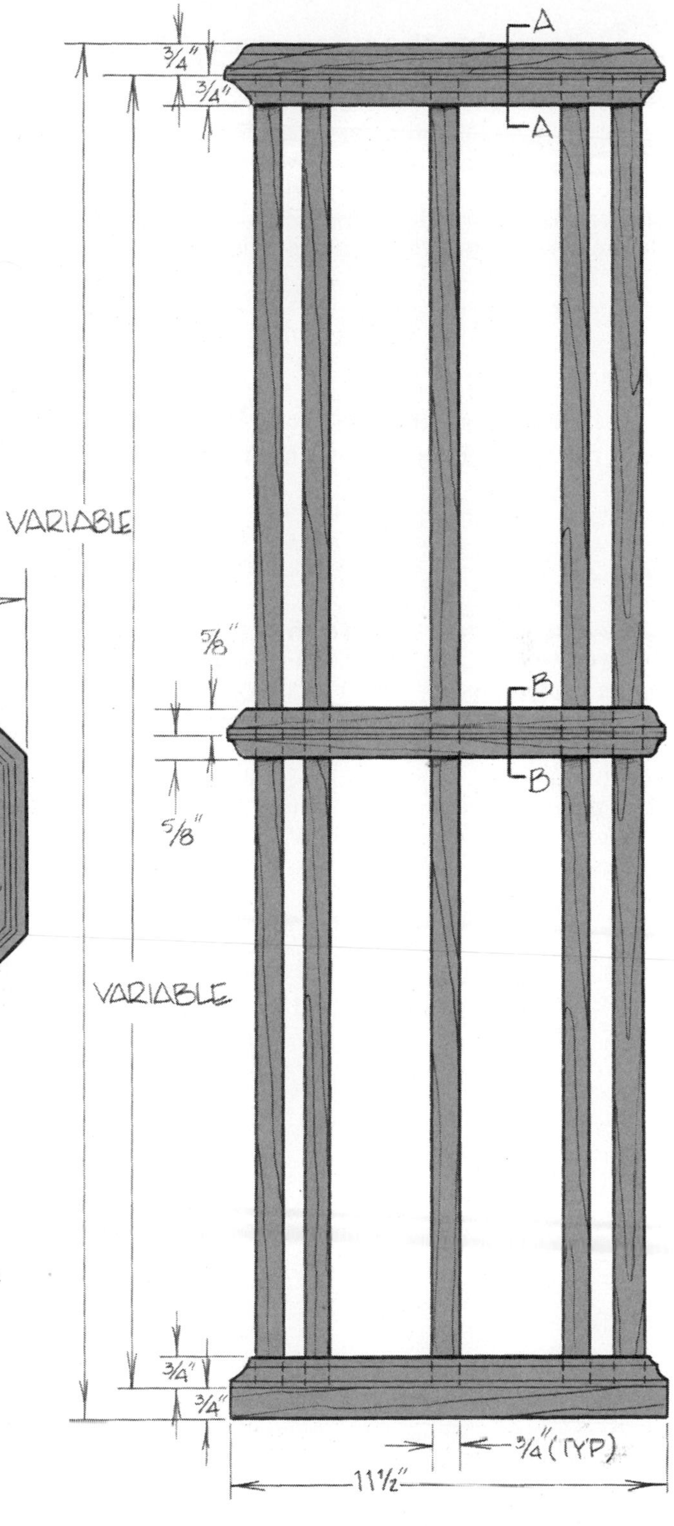
A
A
¾"
¾"
VARIABLE
⅝"
B
B
⅝"
VARIABLE
¾"
¾"
¾" (TYP)
11½"

SIDE VIEW

5

Assemble the stand. Finish sand all the parts. Using waterproof resorcinol or epoxy glue, laminate the paired tops, bottoms, and rings face to face. When gluing the rings together, remember to line up the holes that you marked earlier.

If you want to anchor this stand in place, drill a 1/2"-diameter hole through the center of the bottoms, as shown in the *Top/Bottom Layout.* If you're mounting

a birdbath, sundial, or similar decoration to the stand, you may also want to drill holes through the tops.

Glue the dowels in the bottom assembly. Slide the ring assembly over the dowels, then glue the top assembly in place. Once again, remember to align the marked holes! Slide the ring halfway down the length of the dowels and secure it with finishing nails. Set the heads of the nails.

6

Finish the stand. Do any necessary touch-up sanding, then apply a finish to the completed stand. Use a weatherproof finish such as spar varnish, tung oil, or exterior paint.

7

Anchor the stand to the ground (optional). If you want to fasten the stand permanently in place, pour a small concrete pad 12" round and 4" deep. Set the anchor bolt in the concrete so about 2½" of its length shows. (See Figure 1.)

Let the concrete cure completely (about 48 hours). Place the stand on the pad, inserting the anchor bolt through the hole in the bottom. Put a washer and a nut on the bolt, and tighten the nut.

1/To anchor the stand permanently to the ground, first pour a small concrete pad. Set an anchor bolt in the center of this pad, then fasten the stand to the bolt.

Specialty Hinges

Most projects with a door or a lid also require hinges. Depending on the project, these may be *specialty hinges* — hinges with a specific design or capability. In fact, the design of the hinges may make the project possible. The Bathroom Cabinets in this book are one example. Each cabinet is a box designed to be sandwiched together with other boxes. Because the boxes are attached side by side, each door must pivot so it won't hit or rub the doors to the left or right. Ordinary butt hinges won't do; the pivot is in the wrong place. So the Materials List specifies specialty hinges — European-style *cabinet hinges (A)*. Without these, you would have to hang the cabinets separately.

There are many, many specialty hinges available to woodworkers. Here are a few of the most common.

Double-action hinges (B) swing both ways — in *and* out. To do this, each hinge has several pivot pins.

No-mortise hinges (C) require no mortises yet look like ordinary butt hinges when they're installed. The leaves are just 1/16" thick and they're inset — one leaf folds inside the other.

Concealed hinges (D) are completely hidden from view. You can't even see the pivot when the door is closed. These are normally mounted in holes or slots in the wood.

Knife hinges (E) displace the pivot slightly in front of, behind, or to one side of the door. This helps the door to clear obstacles that might otherwise be in the way if the door were mounted on ordinary hinges. These knife hinges are usually mounted to the top and bottom of the door.

Wraparound hinges (F) have one or more bent leaves that wrap around the wood on the door or door frame. These are useful when you're working with plywood, since hinge screws won't hold securely when driven into the plywood's edge. These hinges let you drive the screws into the face.

Separable hinges (G) come apart. One leaf and the pivot pin lift out of the other leaf. This allows you to detach the door from the project quickly and easily. Gravity keeps the leaves of the hinges together when the door is mounted.

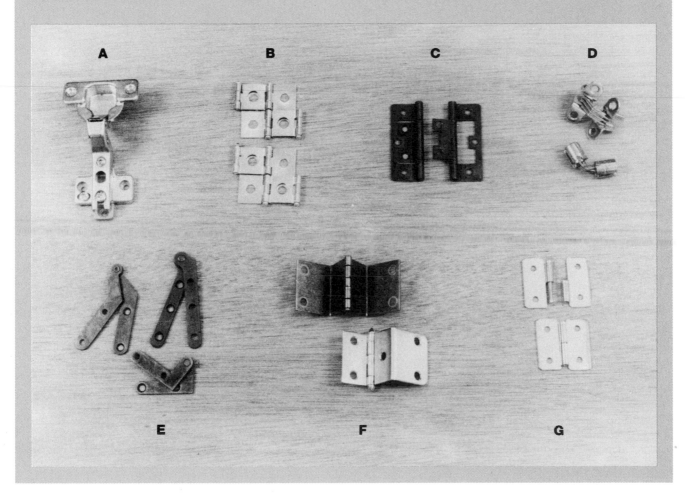

Step-Back Hutch

During medieval times, it became customary for a nobleman to display his "plate," or dinnerware, on open shelves. These shelves were known by several names — cupboard, dresser, buffet, and *hutch*. Often, the number of shelves in a hutch showed the rank of the owner. Squires had but two shelves, lords had three, and so on. Six or more shelves were reserved for royalty.

As the Dark Ages gave way to the Renaissance, dishes and shelving became more broadly popular. Soon, even common folk displayed their dinnerware. The number of shelves in a hutch lost their significance — but the shelves retained their usefulness. Open shelving units were built to hold dishes in both Europe and America well into the nineteenth century. And they continue to be useful, not just for dinnerware, but also for books, collectibles, and any number of small and medium-sized items.

The hutch shown is patterned after country pieces made in New York and Pennsylvania during the mid-eighteenth century. It's called a step-back hutch because the top section is narrower than the bottom and seems to step back toward the wall.

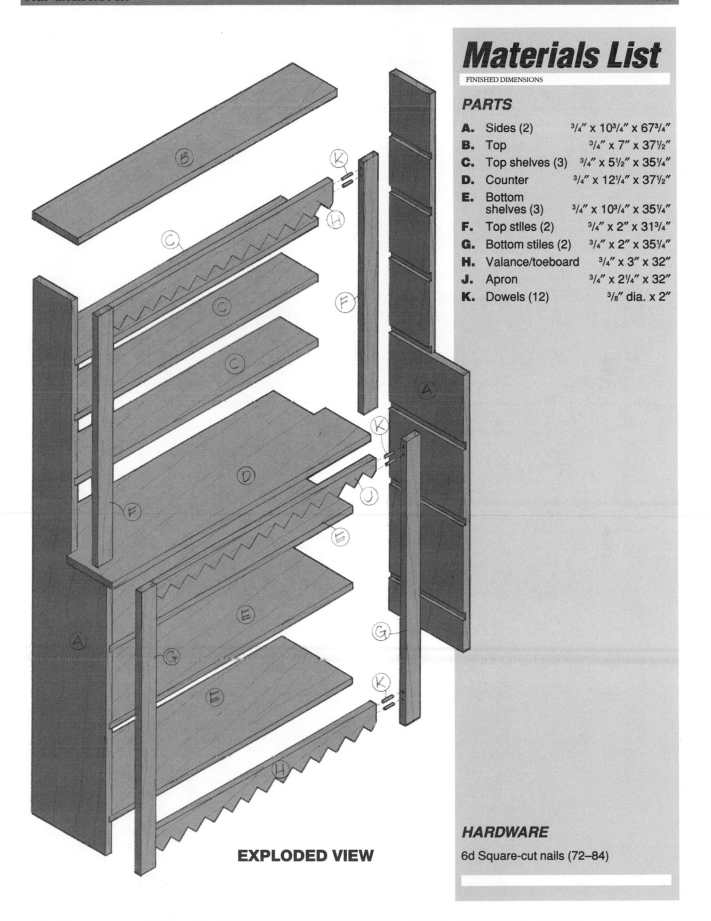

EXPLODED VIEW

Materials List
FINISHED DIMENSIONS

PARTS

A.	Sides (2)	³/₄″ x 10³/₄″ x 67³/₄″
B.	Top	³/₄″ x 7″ x 37½″
C.	Top shelves (3)	³/₄″ x 5½″ x 35¼″
D.	Counter	³/₄″ x 12¼″ x 37½″
E.	Bottom shelves (3)	³/₄″ x 10³/₄″ x 35¼″
F.	Top stiles (2)	³/₄″ x 2″ x 31³/₄″
G.	Bottom stiles (2)	³/₄″ x 2″ x 35¼″
H.	Valance/toeboard	³/₄″ x 3″ x 32″
J.	Apron	³/₄″ x 2¼″ x 32″
K.	Dowels (12)	³/₈″ dia. x 2″

HARDWARE

6d Square-cut nails (72–84)

1

Select the stock and cut it to size. To build this project, you need approximately 36 board feet of 4/4 (four-quarters) lumber. You can use any cabinet-grade hardwood or softwood, although you may want to use an inexpensive wood if you plan to paint the completed project. The hutch shown is made of #2 poplar and finished with latex paint. Many antique hutches were made from walnut, cherry, or maple.

Plane all the lumber to ¾" thick and glue up the stock needed for the wide parts — sides, counter, and bottom shelves. Then cut all the parts to the sizes shown in the Materials List.

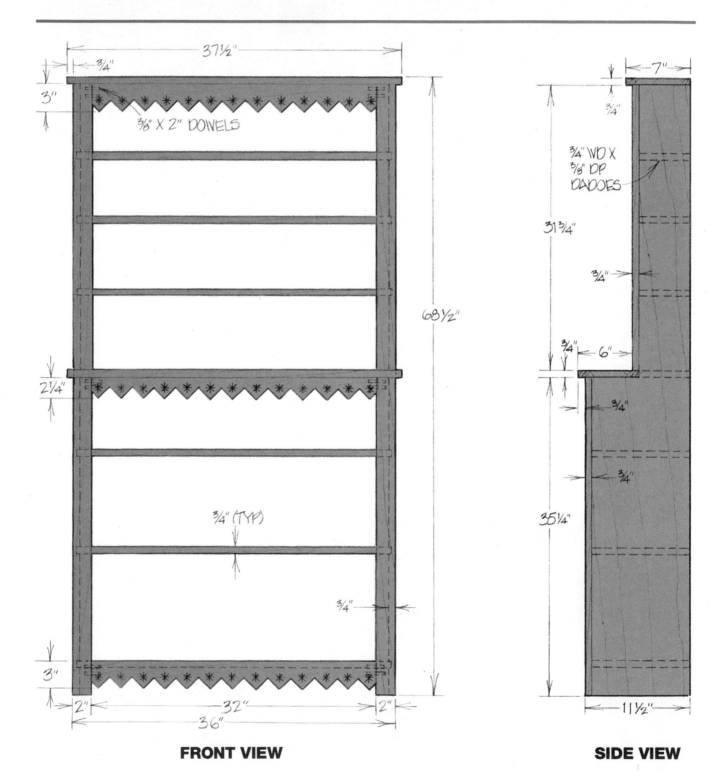

FRONT VIEW   **SIDE VIEW**

2 **Cut the dadoes in the sides.** The shelves and counter rest in ³⁄₄″-wide, ³⁄₈″-deep dadoes in the sides. Place the two sides edge to edge, lining up the ends of each board so the ends are flush. Lay out the dadoes with a T-square or carpenter's square, drawing the lines across *both* sides. This will assure that both sides are marked the same.

Cut the dadoes with a router or a dado cutter. If you use a router, clamp a straightedge to the sides to guide it.

TRY THIS! To quickly rout dadoes in wide boards, make a T-square jig from a few scraps of plywood. Be sure the cross (or short piece) of the T is *precisely* 90° from the leg (long piece). Rout grooves in the cross on both sides of the leg. These grooves must be the same width as the dadoes you want to cut.

To use the jig, place the cross against the edge of the board, and line up one of the grooves with the layout lines for the dadoes. Clamp the T-square to the board and rout the dado, using the leg to guide the router.

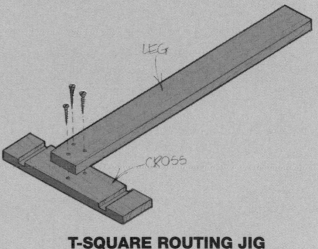

T-SQUARE ROUTING JIG

3 **Cut the shapes of the sides and the counter.** Both the sides and the counter are notched — one or more corners is removed. Lay out the shapes on the stock, as shown in the *Side Layout* or *Counter Layout*. Cut the shapes with a table saw and saber saw. (See Figures 1 and 2.)

1/When cutting the shapes of the sides and the counter, you must make the cuts as straight as possible. Cut as much as you can with a table saw, using the fence or miter gauge to guide the work.

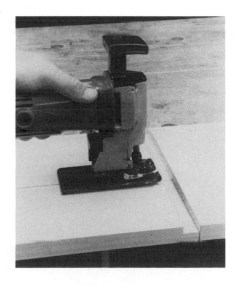

2/Finish up the cuts with a saber saw, taking care to follow the layout lines as precisely as possible. You may want to cut a little wide of the lines, then file away the wood up to them.

4 **Drill the dowel holes in the stiles, valance, apron, and toeboard.** The parts of the face frames — stiles, valance, apron, and toeboard — are all joined with dowels. Using a doweling jig, drill ⅜"-diameter, 1"-deep dowel holes in the inside edges of the stiles and the ends of the other parts. Dry assemble the parts to check the fit of the dowel joints. There should be two dowels per joint, as shown in the *Front View*.

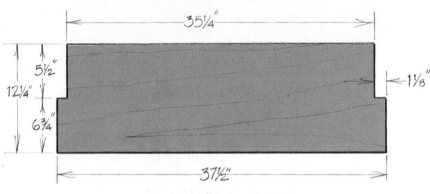

COUNTER LAYOUT

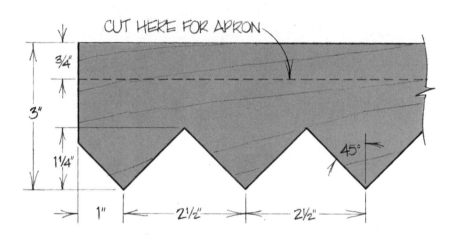

VALANCE/APRON/TOEBOARD LAYOUT

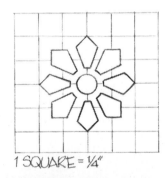

1 SQUARE = ¼"

STENCIL PATTERN
(FULL SIZE)

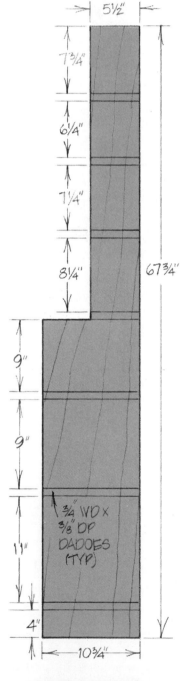

SIDE LAYOUT

5

Cut the shapes of the valance, apron, and toeboard. Lay out the shape of the apron on the *apron* stock, as shown in the *Valance/Apron/Toeboard Layout*. Stack the apron, valance, and toeboard stock with the apron on top. Make sure all the *bottom* edges are flush, then tack the stack together with two 6d finishing nails. Using a band saw or a saber saw, cut the shapes of all three boards at once. (See Figure 3.) Sand the cut edges smooth, remove the finishing nails, and separate the parts.

3/To save time and assure that the shaped parts match, stack the apron, valance, and toeboard. Nail the boards together to keep them from shifting, then cut and sand the shapes in all three parts at once.

6

Assemble the hutch. Finish sand all the parts. Glue together the sides, top shelves, bottom shelves, and counter. Reinforce the glue joints with square-cut nails, driving the nails through the sides and into the ends of the shelves.

Note: To install a square-cut nail, first drill a pilot hole. (The hole diameter should match the width of the shank as measured *halfway* along its length.) This will prevent the nail from splitting the wood. Angle the pilot hole slightly so the nail will not be perpendicular with the surface of the wood. Drive the nail until the square head is flush with the surface of the wood, but do *not* set the nail. (See Figure 4.) Angle the next pilot hole (and nail) in the *opposite* direction, and continue to alternate the angle of each successive nail. This will prevent the boards from pulling apart.

Assemble the top stiles, bottom stiles, valance, apron, and toeboard with glue and dowels, making two separate frames. Before the glue dries, glue the frames to the hutch. Check that the hutch is square, then reinforce the glue joints with square-cut nails.

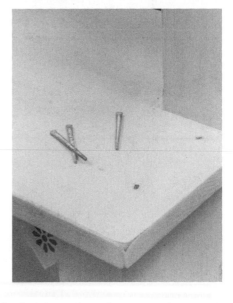

*4/Because they have square heads, square-cut nails look similar to old-time hand-forged nails and give your project a "country" look. Do **not** set the nail heads or cover them with putty — let them show.*

Glue the top to the hutch, and reinforce it with square-cut nails. Let the glue dry completely, then sand all glue joints clean and flush.

7

Finish the hutch. Do any necessary touch-up sanding, then apply a finish to the completed hutch. If you wish to duplicate the aged milk paint finish shown here, follow this procedure:

■ Apply two coats of *flat* latex paint. Choose a warm, "antique" color. Also paint a few scraps — you'll need these as test pieces later on.

■ If you wish, apply a stenciled design to the valance, apron, and toeboard, as shown in the *Front View* and the *Stencil Pattern*. (See Figures 5 and 6.) You may also create your own stencil pattern.

■ Sand the paint down to the bare wood in areas where an old hutch would have seen a lot of wear — the corners, the bottom edge of the toeboard, the fronts of the shelves and counter, and the top. Don't remove a lot of paint, just enough to make the hutch look old.

◼ Distress the surface, adding some dents that a hutch would have accumulated with age. (See Figure 7.) Don't go overboard — just make a few dents here and there. The hutch should look old, not as if it has been through a war.

◼ Apply a mixture of mineral spirits and dark oil-based stain. (Experiment on the test pieces with differ-

ent spirits/stain mixes until you get the effect you want. You may also substitute artist's oils for stain.) Before the mixture dries, wipe most of it off with a rag. This mixture will darken the wood where it shows through the paint. It will also remain in the dents, looking like years of accumulated grime. And it will mute the color of the paint, making it look aged.

◼ Let the spirits/stain mixture dry completely. Then rub down the entire project with dark paste wax.

5/To apply a stenciled pattern, first cut a stencil. You can use Mylar plastic film or special stencil paper to make the stencil. The plastic film is available at most drafting supply stores, and the paper at most arts and crafts supply stores.

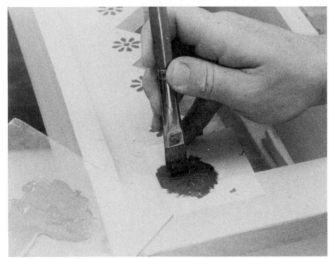

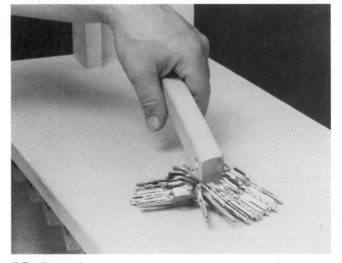

*6/Apply spray adhesive to the back of the stencil and stick it to the project. Dip a stiff brush in artist's acrylic paint, then wipe most of the paint off the brush. (This is what artists call a "dry" brush.) Dab (**don't** wipe) the color onto the voids in the pattern,*

taking care not to apply too much at one time — you don't want the paint to bleed under the stencil. When you're done, peel up the stencil, and stick it down in another place, and repeat the process. If the stencil loses its tack, spray it with more adhesive.

*7/To distress the surface of the hutch, **lightly** beat the project with a collection of old keys. These will make small, subtle dents, nicks, and scratches — the same sort of damage that would have happened to the hutch with the passing of time.*

Credits

About the Author: Nick Engler is a contributing editor to *American Woodworker* magazine and teaches cabinetmaking at the University of Cincinnati. He has written over 20 books on woodworking.

Contributing Craftsmen and Craftswomen:

Larry Callahan (Garden Stand)

Woody Cannell (Collapsible Candleholder)

Doug Crowell (Christmas Crèche)

Judy Ditmer (Turned Boxes)

Nick Engler (Floor-to-Ceiling Bookshelves, Accent Table, Bathroom Cabinets, Compound-Cut Reindeer, Doll Cradle, Glazed Wall Cabinet, Recycling Bins, Shaker Clock)

Mary Jane Favorite (Letter Box, Turkey Whirligig, Step-Back Hutch, Nesting Doves Peg Rack)

Christine Vogel (Fireman's Ladder)

Chris Walendzak (Gravity Bookend)

Special Thanks To:

Gordon Honeyman
Fred and Becky Sacks
Geneva Watts
The Gingerbread House, West Milton, Ohio
Heartwoods, Tipp City, Ohio
Trudy's Florist, West Milton, Ohio
Wertz Hardware Store, West Milton, Ohio

Rodale Press, Inc., publishes AMERICAN WOODWORKER™, the magazine for the serious woodworking hobbyist. For information on how to order your subscription, write to AMERICAN WOODWORKER™, Emmaus, PA 18098.

WOODWORKING GLOSSARY

Parts of a Board

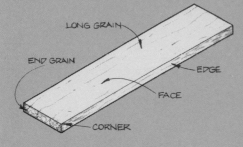

LONG GRAIN
END GRAIN
EDGE
FACE
CORNER

Basic Saw Cuts

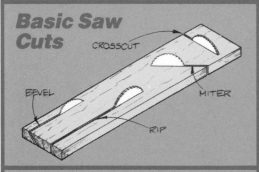

CROSSCUT
BEVEL
MITER
RIP

Parts of a Drawer

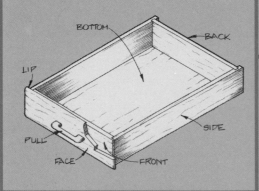

BOTTOM
BACK
LIP
SIDE
PULL
FACE
FRONT

Parts of a Frame

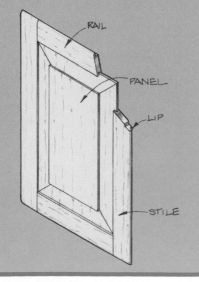

RAIL
PANEL
LIP
STILE

Basic Joinery

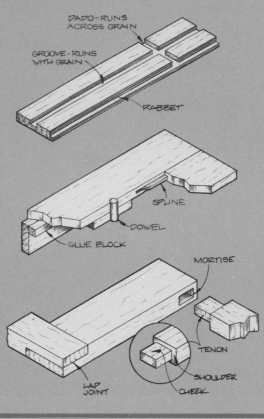

DADO - RUNS ACROSS GRAIN
GROOVE - RUNS WITH GRAIN
RABBET
SPLINE
DOWEL
GLUE BLOCK
MORTISE
TENON
LAP JOINT
SHOULDER
CHEEK

Parts of a Tabl[e]

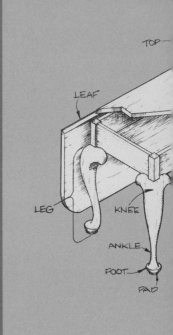

TOP
LEAF
LEG
KNEE
ANKLE
FOOT
PAD

Common Shapes and Moldings

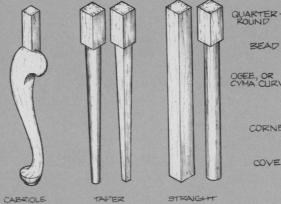
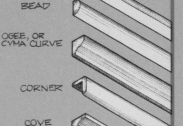

CABRIOLE
TAPER
STRAIGHT

QUARTER-ROUND
BEAD
OGEE, OR CYMA CURVE
CORNER
COVE
BED
CROWN

Holes

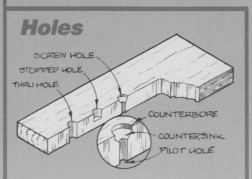

SCREW HOLE
STOPPED HOLE
THRU HOLE
COUNTERBORE
COUNTERSINK
PILOT HOLE

Pa[rts]

FACE FRAME
WEB FRAME
SHELF SUPPORT
BASE

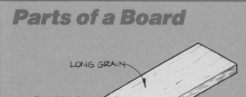